AMERICA IN THE 1930s

JIM CALLAN

Facts On File, Inc.

To my nephew Leo, a great future writer

A Stonesong Press Book
Decades of American History: *America in the 1930s*

Facts On File, Inc.
132 West 31st Street
New York NY 10001

  Library of Congress Cataloging-in-Publication Data

Callan, Jim.
  America in the 1930s / Jim Callan.
        p. cm. — (Decades of American history)
  "A Stonesong Press book."
  Includes bibliographical references and index.
  ISBN 0-8160-5638-2
1. United States—History—1933–1945—Juvenile literature. 2. United
States—History—1919–1933—Juvenile literature. 3. Nineteen
thirties—Juvenile literature. I. Title. II. Series.
  E806.C316 2005
  973.917—dc22

                                        2004018949

Facts On File books are available at special discounts when purchaed in bulk quantities
for businesses, associations, institutions, or sales promotions. Please call our Special Sales
Department in New York at (212) 967-8800 or (800) 322-8755.

You can find Facts On File on the World Wide Web at http://www.factsonfile.com

Text design by Laura Smyth, Smythetype
Photo research by Larry Schwartz
Cover design by Pehrsson Design

Printed in the United States of America

VB PKG 10 9 8 7 6 5 4 3 2 1

This book is printed on acid-free paper.

CONTENTS

CHAPTER 1

AMERICA IN 1930, THE DEPRESSION BEGINS

THE 1930s PRESENTED THE UNITED STATES with some of the toughest challenges it had ever faced. The decade started with a prolonged economic depression and ended with the start of World War II. In between, organized crime took advantage of the new nationwide prohibition laws banning the manufacture and sale of alcohol. Criminals controlled its illegal sale and rose to great power throughout the country's urban areas, and notorious bank robbers terrorized many rural areas. Once-fertile farmland in Texas, Oklahoma, Kansas, Colorado, and New Mexico was so damaged by soil erosion and drought that the area became known as the dust bowl. Labor disputes turned America's streets into bloody battlegrounds between striking workers and management's strikebreakers.

U.S. farms were hit by hard times starting in the 1920s. Farm product prices plummeted 40 percent between 1920 and 1921 as overseas markets disappeared. This contributed to the depression of the 1930s. *(Library of Congress)*

Evacuation sales were common during the depression as banks foreclosed on bankrupt households. By 1933, 300,000 families had lost their homes. *(Franklin D. Roosevelt Presidential Library and Museum)*

On February 18, 1930, astronomer Clyde Tombaugh first photographed the ninth planet of the solar system. The planet was later named Pluto after the Roman god of the underworld.

Of all the problems the United States faced during the 1930s, however, the Great Depression caused the most widespread hardships. Starting with the stock market crash on Black Thursday, October 24, 1929, America's economy declined into chaos. Personal fortunes were wiped out, banks failed, unemployment soared, and families struggled just to survive. Many Americans started to lose faith in their government, and some lost confidence in the American way of life.

The roots of the Great Depression go back to the early 1920s. On the surface, it seemed as if America were enjoying a time of great prosperity. Unemployment was at an all-time low. More and more people bought and used the products of modern technology, such as refrigerators and automobiles. Automobile ownership nearly tripled during the 1920s, from 8 million cars in 1920 to 23 million by 1929. Radio was becoming a big part of Americans' lives, offering music, entertainment, and news. The decade also saw weekly movie attendance double from 40 million to 80 million as Americans flocked to palatial new movie theaters. Despite Prohibition (the era when alcohol manufacture and sale was illegal), American youth were having the party of their lives, often in speakeasies where illegal liquor could be bought. Feeling prosperous was made easy with installment or credit buying, which allowed consumers to buy almost anything they wanted with just a small down payment and the balance due in future monthly payments. The decade became known as the Roaring Twenties.

Beneath the surface, however, were warning signs that few seemed to care about. One hint that the economy was in trouble was the drop in the construction of new homes. Home building, a common indicator of economic strength, sharply declined from 1926 to 1929.

The clearest measure of the declining economy was in U.S. farming. During World War I, U.S. farmers prospered, as war-torn European nations needed U.S.-grown produce and there was great demand. The result was a tremendous increase in agricultural production, income, and purchasing power. Many farmers used the profits of this farming boom to invest in more land and more machinery.

After the war, however, prices and profits plummeted as the European market no longer purchased U.S. food products. When World War I began, the federal government had guaranteed U.S. farmers minimum prices on certain crops. But in 1921, President Warren Harding announced the end of these crop price supports. In 1923, President Calvin Coolidge raised taxes on imports, which decreased American foreign trade and took away more of the farmers' markets. It was all a disaster for the farmers. Many were forced into bankruptcy, and others lost their new land investments to bank foreclosures. (A foreclosure happens when a bank borrower is unable to pay back a loan. The bank then takes possession of whatever the borrower bought with the loan—a house, land, a car, or tractor, and so on.)

The other problem with the U.S. economy came from a business practice that became very common in the 1920s. Not only did the U.S. public buy products on credit, but banks also used credit to make investments. Business leaders urged President Coolidge to give credit to banks to fuel the nation's economy. The banks used some of this credit to issue loans to investors and encouraged them to use installment buying to increase the number of their investments. The usual investments were in real estate and a newly flourishing arena, the stock market. The result of all this borrowing and spending was an economy that seemed to be booming with an unlimited amount of money. It was

By 1930, 80 percent of all cars bought in America were bought on credit.

In 1929, General Motors Company stock sold for $91 a share. In 1932, it was selling for only $7 a share. In 1929, U.S. Steel stock sold for $261 a share. In 1932, it had dropped to $21 a share.

Calvin Coolidge said, "The chief business of the American people is business," but poor business practices during his presidency led in part to the Great Depression. *(Library of Congress)*

a false prosperity, however, because it was not based on real money. It was based on the promised money of loans, and eventually all loans need to be repaid.

The area where installment buying proved most disastrous was the stock market. Then, as is true today, businesses raised money by issuing their stocks for sale to investors. Depending upon how well the business did, the value of the stock rose or fell. If the business was successful and had profits, it paid its investors a dividend, which was like interest on a loan, and the value of the stock rose. If the business was not successful, it either issued more stock to raise more money, or it failed, causing investors to lose their money.

In the 1920s, no one seemed to believe that any business could fail. Investors kept purchasing millions of dollars' worth of stocks, which drove the prices higher and higher. This rise in prices gave the appearance of great business profits, and new millionaires were made every day. More and more people started buying stocks, often investing their life earnings. Most stock market investors were buying on credit, or on margin as it is called in the stock market, borrowing from their stockbrokers, who usually gave them large amounts of credit. Most investors also expected they would get rich quick.

By 1927, some economists were concerned for three reasons. First, many of the businesses in which people were buying stock were of questionable value. These businesses had been formed in order to sell stock and make a quick profit. Investors were so anxious to get involved in the market, they did not take the time to learn anything about these companies before buying their stock. Unscrupulous brokers would often push investors to buy the stock of these new companies just to make a sale. Second, speculators—stockholders who sell off their stock once it reaches a higher value—were cashing in their stocks, thereby withdrawing whatever real money the market had. The buy-today-sell-tomor-

As the depression grew worse, the poorest Americans had no money for food. Many stood in breadlines for hours for a free meal. *(Franklin D. Roosevelt Presidential Library and Museum)*

row practice of the speculators was particularly harmful because a healthy stock market depends on long-term investment. Third, it was becoming clear that both the stockbrokers and banks that had loaned so much money were overextended, lending more money than could be repaid. By 1929, stockbrokers had borrowed $6 billion from banks. If these loans became due, the brokers would not be able to pay most of them off.

To stem the tide, the economists called on the government agency called the Federal Reserve Board, or Fed, to raise interest rates. The Fed controls the amount of money circulating in the U.S. economy. It lends money to banks at a certain interest rate. If the interest rate is high, banks will borrow less money and therefore loan out less money. The Fed raised the interest rates twice, but it had no effect. The Fed also forbade banks from using their money on speculation in the market. This also had little effect; the economic system was out of control.

"Yes, it was called the Dark Ages and it lasted 400 years."

—Economist John Maynard Keynes, when asked if the world had ever seen anything like the Great Depression

"We are the first nation in the history of the world to go to the poorhouse in an automobile."

—American humorist
Will Rogers

In 1930, Sinclair Lewis became the first American writer to win the Nobel Prize for literature. He was awarded the prize based on all of his published writings, which included the well-known novel *Babbitt.*

THE BIG CRASH

In September 1929, prices in the stock market began to drop steadily. Investors had seen prices decrease before, and the market bounced back quickly, but not this time. Prices continued to drop throughout October until October 24, a day that became known as Black Thursday. That morning, a flood of selling began on the floor of the New York Stock Exchange. It is generally believed that brokers started the wave of selling because they needed cash to pay back their loans. When investors saw stock prices dropping, they started selling, too. The floor of the Stock Exchange was soon in a panic. By midday, the prices of many stocks were half of what they had been the day before. The more prices plummeted, the more investors sold off their stocks. At 12:30 P.M., the Exchange closed its visitors' gallery. Outside the building, a huge crowd gathered on Wall Street. The Stock Exchange had already lost $4 billion.

That afternoon, some of the nation's most powerful bankers, including J. P. Morgan, met to try to stem the tide. Many of them had their fortunes tied up in the stock market. The bankers decided to pool $40 million and immediately buy stock. They hoped that the influx of money would stabalize prices so that investors would stop selling. The strategy worked for a couple of days and the market settled down, but on Monday, October 28, the selling frenzy began again. This time, the bankers did not come to the rescue. On Black Tuesday, October 29, more than 16 million shares of stock were sold. By the end of the day, many stocks were virtually worthless. Altogether, stock prices declined by over $10 billion. Entire fortunes were wiped out, and many millionaires became penniless overnight.

By the end of 1929, stockholders had lost $40 billion in the stock market crash, but that was just the beginning. The crash had a ripple effect on the U.S. economy that led to the Great Depression, affecting millions of Americans. Companies now had no money to

COLLECT $200 FOR PASSING GO

In 1932, Charles Darrow of Germantown, Pennsylvania, was one of America's unemployed. He loved board games, so he decided to invent one of his own. Since the depression was on everyone's mind, Darrow wanted a game about money and property investment. He based his game on a couple of investment games that he had played locally. He came up with one of the most popular board games ever invented, Monopoly. In Monopoly, fortunes are easily won or lost with the roll of the dice as players invest their money in property development. For the names of the properties in the game, Darrow chose actual street names and places, such as Boardwalk and Park Place,

in Atlantic City, New Jersey, a popular seaside resort where he had vacationed years before.

When Darrow took his idea to a game manufacturer named Parker Brothers, he was told it was too complicated and dull. Darrow still thought he had a great game, so he borrowed some money and had 5,000 games made up himself. He convinced some department stores in Philadelphia to stock the game, and it started selling immediately. Parker Brothers heard of the sales and contacted Darrow. The company agreed to manufacture the game, and Charles Darrow became a millionaire, the first man to become rich from a board game.

The boardwalk in Atlantic City, New Jersey, became a symbol of wealth in the popular board game Monopoly. *(Library of Congress)*

conduct business, so they laid off workers. Within a few months of the crash, more than 4 million Americans were unemployed. Thousands of companies went out of business because many Americans did not have the money to buy their goods or services. Unemployment rose to 8 million by mid-1931 and then skyrocketed to 13.5 million by the end of that year. About one-third of the entire American workforce was out of work.

As hunger and starvation became a growing problem, breadlines formed, filled with people waiting for free handouts of soup and bread from charities. Many Americans lost their homes when they could not pay their monthly mortgage installments. A new homeless population moved into city parks and built campfires to stay warm. Some people constructed huts out of cardboard, and others fought over scraps of food that they found in garbage cans. Some wandered the country as

One of the few businesses that flourished during 1930 was the manufacture of glass jars. During the depression in order to save money, many families prepared fruits and other foods for long-term storage by boiling them with sugar to preserve them and sealing them in glass jars.

Unemployment reached 13 million at the height of the depression. Here, one of America's unemployed sells apples on a street corner. *(AP/Wide World)*

"All you have to do to win is stay alive."

—Vice-presidential candidate James Garner to presidential candidate Franklin D. Roosevelt after the 1932 Democratic National Convention

America's homeless built shantytowns on the outskirts of cities or along roadways. The areas were plagued by crime, hunger, and disease. *(Franklin D. Roosevelt Presidential Library and Museum)*

hoboes searching desperately for any work at all. One estimate put the number of drifters in America in 1931 at 1 million, with 100,000 of them children. In New York City, a dramatic symbol of the depression appeared as 6,000 apple sellers set up stands on the streets and tried to survive by selling apples for five cents each.

The crash was a disaster for banks. Their loans to investors and brokers were not repaid, leaving them short of cash. As bank customers learned of the cash shortage, they scrambled to withdraw their savings. Once the cash was gone, the banks had no choice but to close their doors. In 1930, banks were closing at the rate of 50 to 60 a day, wiping out the lifetime savings of many Americans.

To make matters worse, the United States of the early 1930s had no government social programs to ease the hardships. There was no unemployment insurance, no Social Security, no Medicare, and no food stamps. The only help available was from local governments and charities such as the Red Cross and the Salvation Army. Unfortunately, they, too, began to run out of money by the end of 1931. The mood of America was so hopeless, the birth rate dropped for the first time in many years, as people put off having children they could not afford.

"THERE ISN'T ANY ONE OF YOU GETTING OUT OF HERE ALIVE"

One of the horrible ironies of the Great Depression was the withholding and even destruction of food while so many starved. The cause of the problem was low prices. When it became more expensive for farmers to produce their food than to sell it, many farmers became desperate. They formed groups called Farm Holiday Associations to stop selling their food until prices were forced higher. Their motto became "Neither buy nor sell and let the taxes go to hell."

The farmers formed picket lines that blocked major highways in the nation's farming states. Any farmer who tried to pass to sell his goods was turned back. If anyone resisted, the Farm Holiday farmers used their pitchforks to disable the tires of their vehicles. Some protestors overturned milk wagons and dumped the milk into ditches. Back on the farm, surpluses of crops such as wheat and corn lay rotting in silos. Stockyards were emptied of livestock and shut down.

One group of farmers, desperate to sell crops, hired local deputies to protect them from the Farm Holiday roadblocks and get their produce to market. Their convoy of trucks came up to one lone Holiday farmer who had placed some nailed planks across the road. A deputy told the Farm Holiday farmer to remove the planks or he would be shot. The farmer said, "Go ahead and shoot, but there isn't any one of you getting out of here alive if you do." Fifteen hundred Farm Holiday farmers came out of the woods along the highway pointing guns at the deputies. The deputies turned the trucks around.

Farm Holiday Associations tried to raise the price of their products by preventing their sale. Some farmers destroyed their own crops out of desperation. *(Library of Congress)*

The farmers' depression started in 1921 when President Harding ended farm price supports. As prices plummeted, many farmers went bankrupt and could not pay their mortgages. *(Franklin D. Roosevelt Presidential Library and Museum)*

THE FARMERS

The stock market crash of 1929 was the most dramatic event contributing to the causes of the Great Depression. Although billions of dollars were lost overnight, shattering confidence in America's economic future, in 1929, only 1.5 million Americans were actually involved enough in the stock market to have a broker. On the other hand, the 40 million Americans living on farms had been enduring a depression since 1919. In the wake of the crash, they would be the hardest hit again, particularly those in the farming states of the Great Plains.

Throughout the 1920s, overproduction led to food prices so low that farmers lost money by simply harvesting their crops. Foreclosures on farmland and machinery were already common in the 1920s. By the early 1930s, 25 percent of farms were being lost to foreclosure. In a desperate attempt to make prices rise, farmers destroyed their own crops, dumped their milk onto the ground, and destroyed their livestock. Yet prices kept dropping. Only the farmers knew it, but the depression had already started before the Big Crash of 1929.

"If they come to take my farm, I'm going to fight. I'd rather be killed than die by starvation. But before I die, I'm going to set fire to my crops, I'm going to burn my house, I'm going to poison my cattle."

—A Great Plains farmer facing foreclosure

CHAPTER 2

HARD TIMES, 1930–1932

President Hoover was blamed for much of the suffering during the depression. Shantytowns and tent cities such as this one were often called Hoovervilles. *(Franklin D. Roosevelt Presidential Library and Museum)*

THROUGHOUT THE 1920S, NEITHER President Warren Harding nor President Calvin Coolidge foresaw the economic disaster coming. The leading economists of the day thought the economy was strong and would remain so well into the 1930s. Business was being conducted in new ways, especially in the stock market, and it would have been difficult for either president to predict all the consequences during their terms of office. However, the severe problems of the American farmer were very clear, and neither Harding nor Coolidge made any real effort to deal with that issue.

In 1932, American aviator Amelia Earhart became the first woman to fly solo across the Atlantic Ocean.

"We in America today are nearer to the final triumph over poverty than ever before in the history of any land."

—Herbert Hoover, as he accepted the Republican nomination for the presidency in 1928

The 1928 presidential election took place during a time that appeared to be very prosperous. The nation's gross national product was at an all-time high, and the stock market was soaring. Because both Harding and Coolidge were Republicans, it seemed certain that the Republican nominee, Secretary of Commerce Herbert Hoover, would win easily.

Hoover was an engineer, businessman, and self-made millionaire. He came to prominence during World War I as the U.S. food administrator under President Woodrow Wilson. His organizational skills helped feed millions in war-torn Europe. As secretary of commerce under both Harding and Coolidge, Hoover's accomplishments included bringing regulations to the new radio broadcasting industry, developing commercial aviation, and eliminating the 12-hour workday in the steel industry.

American voters in 1928 wanted to keep America prosperous. The election was a landslide for Hoover. He defeated the Democratic nominee, New York governor Alfred E. Smith, 444 electoral votes to 87, carrying 40 of the 48 states. It was the largest margin of victory ever achieved by a presidential candidate up until that time.

HOOVER'S POLICIES

One of Hoover's first acts as president was his signing of the Agricultural Marketing Act, a bill to deal with the agricultural depression. The bill offered loans to farmers and encouraged farming cooperatives. (In a farming cooperative, the farmers act together in economic activities rather than in competition with each other.) The bill was a failure. Many leaders in Congress believed the farming economy was so weak that only direct government subsidies would help, but Hoover did not believe that government should interfere with business. It was a belief that would doom his presidency to failure.

Children were hit hard by the depression. Fathers often deserted their families in a desperate search for work. *(Library of Congress)*

Seven months after Hoover took office, the stock market crashed. Hoover believed the stock market would eventually recover and that the American economy would be unaffected. As the ripple effect from the stock market crash led the United States into the Great Depression, Hoover still refused to intervene. He encouraged business leaders to take the initiative to get industry moving again and stimulate the economy. He thought as business improved, jobs would be created, and people would have money again. This theory is called "trickle-down economics," and it is how Hoover thought prosperity would return to America.

"I do not believe that the power and duty of the general government ought to be extended to the relief of individual suffering."

—President Herbert Hoover in 1930

Representative W. C. Hawley (left) and Senator Reed Smoot (right) were responsible for the disastrous Hawley-Smoot Tariff Act. The bill hurt the economy by reducing exports. *(Library of Congress)*

In June 1930, Hoover signed the Hawley-Smoot Tariff Act despite a petition from one thousand economists from around the country urging him to veto it. The bill sharply raised tariffs, or fees charged on foreign imports, in order to make U.S. products more competitive. The theory behind tariffs holds that if a foreign product costs more than one made in the United States, consumers will buy U.S. goods. But the economists were right. The bill had the opposite effect and was particularly harmful to the U.S. farmer. The main effect of the bill was to reduce U.S. exports because other nations reacted by raising their tariffs. With even less of a foreign market for their goods, U.S. business declined further. As a direct result of Hawley-Smoot, investments in American businesses with any involvement overseas decreased, and unemployment rose even higher. The higher tariffs also immobilized world trade and helped spread the effects of the depression worldwide.

To Hoover, any intervention from the federal government threatened the foundations of capitalism. As the depression set in, and it became clear that many Americans were becoming homeless and unemployed, Hoover resisted federal government relief. Such programs, he believed, would undermine the initiative and self-respect of Americans and bankrupt the federal government. He said huge federal programs would lead to governmental corruption and waste and do more harm than good in the long run. There were local governments and charities to help the homeless. Besides, prosperity, he told the public, "was just around the corner."

Throughout 1930 and 1931, however, the depression deepened and Hoover's reputation suffered. As America's homeless built shantytowns in the parks and on the outskirts of cities, they became known as

Hoovervilles. Broken-down automobiles pulled by mules were called Hoover wagons. Discarded newspapers that the homeless used to try to stay warm became known as Hoover blankets. The man who had won the presidency in a landslide had quickly became the symbol of what had gone wrong in America.

THE DUST BOWL

Just when farmers thought it could not get any worse, their soil itself became useless to them. For many years, the land of the Great Plains states (Texas, Oklahoma, Missouri, Kansas, Iowa, Nebraska, North Dakota, and South Dakota) was mismanaged. Three big mistakes were made by American farmers. First, they did not practice crop rotation to protect the soil, as European farmers had for more than one hundred years. (Crop

Severe drought and overuse of the land turned the fertile soil of the Great Plains states into dust. High winds blew the dust as far east as the Atlantic Ocean. *(Library of Congress)*

On March 3, 1931, President Hoover signed a bill officially making Francis Scott Key's "The Star Spangled Banner" the national anthem of the United States.

"Once I built a railroad, made it run, made it race against time. Once I built a railroad, now it's done. 'Brother, can you spare a dime?'"

—Lyrics from a popular 1932 song, "Brother, Can You Spare a Dime?"

rotation means that a farmer does not grow the same plant year after year on the same soil. Different plants take different nutrients from the soil, so changing crops gives different types of nutrients the time to build up again.) Second, much of the area's natural grasslands were converted to huge fields of wheat during the early 1900s. The invention of the tractor meant that 50 acres of land could be plowed each day and production could skyrocket, but the absence of natural grasses left the soil vulnerable to wind erosion. Third, the remaining grasslands were destroyed by the overgrazing of livestock, especially cattle and sheep.

Conditions became worse in 1931 when a drought began that lasted seven years. (A drought is a long period of less than normal rainfall.) The dry, windy condi-

Many dust bowl families packed up their cars and sought a better life in California. So many migrants came that local police started turning them back. *(Library of Congress)*

tions turned the once fertile topsoil into dust. It was then blown away in disastrous windstorms called black blizzards. Sometimes, the dust would blow as far east as Washington, D.C., and other East Coast cities. The hardest hit area, centered around the Oklahoma and Texas panhandles, became known as the dust bowl.

As foreclosures increased and farmers abandoned their now worthless land, a mass migration started. During the 1930s, an estimated 3 million people left the Great Plains states in the largest migration in U.S. history. Many people packed up their old trucks and cars and headed west for California where they heard conditions were much better and jobs were available.

So many of the migrants came from Oklahoma that they came to be known as Okies, and what they found was usually more hardship. California farms were highly mechanized and needed few workers to maintain them, so there were many more migrants

Migrants often had little choice but to live in their cars on the way to California. They pulled their automobiles over to the side of the road to use as makeshift homes. *(Franklin D. Roosevelt Presidential Library and Museum)*

"NO PANHANDLING, NO DRINKING, AND NO RADICALISM"

In 1924, veterans of World War I were promised a bonus for their service during the war. Congress said the bonus would be paid in 1945, but the poverty and unemployment of 1932 made many men desperate for their money right away. A group led by Walter Waters was formed in Portland, Oregon, and called the Bonus Expeditionary Force (BEF). The BEF demanded that the bonus be paid immediately.

The BEF decided to publicize its cause by marching on Washington, D.C., and petitioning Congress and President Hoover for the bonuses. To help gain support for their mission, Waters insisted on discipline from the veterans. He told them, "No panhandling [begging], no drinking, and no radicalism [extremism or militancy]."

Veterans and their families from all over the country joined the march. Many hitchhiked; some hopped freight trains. By the time they reached Washington, they numbered more than 20,000 and were called the Bonus Army. They camped wherever they could: in unoccupied federal buildings, on the Capitol lawn, and in a Hooverville that was built on the outskirts of Washington on the Anacostia Flats. Some members of Congress agreed to speak to Bonus Army representatives, but President Hoover would not allow any of them access to the White House.

On June 15, 1932, the House of Representatives passed a bill providing for immediate payment of the bonus, but it still needed the approval of the Senate and President Hoover. Two days later, the Senate voted the bill down. When Waters informed the veterans on the Capitol lawn of the vote, they were stunned. After a moment of silence, they sadly started singing "America."

The veterans started to disperse over the next few days, but about 5,000 stayed behind. They camped mostly in the Hooverville on Anacostia Flats, now called Bonus City. Most of them were homeless and had nowhere to go. Hoover looked upon those who remained as a threat to the government and a vivid reminder to the public of the country's problems. He ordered his Army Chief of Staff, General Douglas MacArthur, to use troops to remove the remaining veterans from Washington, but to leave the veterans in Anacostia Flats alone.

MacArthur ignored Hoover's order and had his troops attack the unarmed veterans in Bonus City with tanks, bayonets, and tear gas. One thousand were injured and two children were killed. The camp was then set on fire by the troops. In explaining why U.S. Army troops attacked the veterans of the Bonus Army, Hoover defended MacArthur and said, "A challenge to the authority of the United States government has been met swiftly and firmly. Our government cannot be coerced by mob rule."

Congress finally voted to pay the veterans their bonuses in 1936.

Veterans hurl stones and bricks at U.S. troops advancing on their Bonus City camp.
(Library of Congress)

than jobs. The only jobs available to the migrants were as pickers. Once-proud farmers who had cultivated many acres of wheat or cotton now worked for pennies a day picking fruits and vegetables.

Migrants who were lucky enough to find work as pickers made their homes in the minimal camp facilities provided by the growers. Thousands of others merely pitched camps on roadsides next to irrigation ditches. Still more gave up and headed for urban areas of California such as Modesto, Fresno, and Bakersfield. No matter where they went, the Okies faced discrimination from local populations. They were looked upon as a drain on the local economy and even as an eyesore. Sometimes roadblocks were set up at the California/Arizona border to turn the Okies back.

HOOVER FINALLY RESPONDS

In February 1932, Hoover finally set up a major federal program to stimulate the economy, the Reconstruction Finance Corporation (RFC). The RFC was empowered to loan $2 billion to railroads, mines, banks, and other financial institutions, such as insurance companies and mortgage loan firms. Many financial institutions were saved by the RFC loans, but little of the money was then invested into the general economy.

At the same time Hoover directed the Federal Farm Board, set up by the Agricultural Marketing Act, to buy up large amounts of farm surpluses to help stabilize crop prices. In June, Hoover signed the Revenue Act of 1932, significantly increasing taxes on corporations and the wealthy. In July, Hoover also signed the Emergency Relief and Construction Act to stimulate the nation's building industry. Through this bill, money was set aside for public works across the country such as the Hoover Dam project on the Arizona-Nevada border. The act also made loans to local governments to subsidize their relief efforts.

ART DECO

Art deco refers to a fresh, streamlined style popular in the 1920s and 1930s. The term comes from the Exposition Internationale des Arts Decoratifs Industriels et Modernes (International Exposition of Decorative, Industrial, and Modern Arts), held in Paris, France, in 1925. Art deco, with its simplified, geometric shapes and patterns, emphasized and celebrated the rise of modern industry and technology. Telephones, jewelry, housewares, cars, furniture, and more were created in the art deco style, which was also reflected in books and newspapers, advertising, and even the design of letters and numbers.

There were more than 200,000 foreclosures on homes, farms, and businesses in 1932.

THE EMPIRE STATE BUILDING

In the late 1920s, America was feeling at its height of optimism and prosperity. Skyscrapers had been rising high above the American landscape since the late 1800s. In 1928, the architect R. H. Shreve decided to build the world's tallest building in New York City. He designed the 102-story, 1,250-foot high Empire State Building, and construction began in 1929 on Fifth Avenue and 34th Street.

A few months later, the stock market crash and the Great Depression hit America. The building's owners had to decide if they wanted to continue the costly construction. They decided to finish building the skyscraper as a symbol of their belief in the nation's future. The Empire State Building opened on May 1, 1931. Visitors stood in line for hours to take the tour of the mighty structure and ride its elevators high into the sky. The tour cost $1, which was a lot of money at the time, but just as the owners hoped, it seemed to give people faith in the future.

With its geometric patterns and streamlined shape, the Empire State Building is an example of a design style that was very popular at the time called art deco. Unfortunately, its 2 million square feet of office space remained mostly vacant for several years after it opened until business recovered from the Great Depression.

Built in less than two years, the Empire State Building set speed records for construction that still stand. Above is a view about halfway through construction. *(Library of Congress)*

These moves, in the final months of Hoover's term, were generally considered to be too little, too late. Right after members of Congress approved the RFC, they also passed a bill authorizing federal relief to the unemployed and homeless, but Hoover vetoed the act. By 1932, the public's frustration and despair were turning to violence. Crowds demanded free food from grocery stores and jobs from factories. In Dearborn, Michigan, 3,000 unemployed men stormed the Ford Motor Company plant to present a petition demanding jobs. The police tried to turn them back with tear gas. When the workers fought back with stones, the police opened fire with guns, killing 4 and wounding 50.

THE CRIME OF THE CENTURY

Prohibition had resulted in a rise in organized crime in America in the 1920s and early 1930s. Americans were used to headlines about rival gangs gunning each other down to control the illegal alcohol business. However, no American was prepared for the news of the tragic kidnapping and murder of aviator Charles Lindbergh's baby in 1932. It is often referred to as the crime of the century.

Charles Lindbergh was America's greatest hero in the early 1930s. His solo flight across the Atlantic Ocean in 1927 was an aviation first and made Lucky Lindy the world's most famous celebrity. On March 1, 1932, his celebrity brought him tragedy when his 20-month old son was kidnapped from the Lindbergh home in New Jersey. A $50,000 ransom was paid, but 10 weeks later the baby was found murdered.

In 1934, a carpenter named Bruno Hauptmann was arrested in New York and charged with the crime after he was found with some of the marked ransom money. Hauptmann was convicted amid complaints of an unfair trial. He was executed in 1936, still protesting his innocence. Lindbergh continued to be so hounded by the press that he moved his family to Europe to find privacy. The crime resulted in the Lindbergh Law, which made kidnapping a federal offense.

Governor Al Smith of New York lost the 1932 Democratic presidential nomination to Franklin Roosevelt. The two later became bitter rivals. *(Library of Congress)*

America was falling apart. Between 1930 and 1932, more than 85,000 businesses had failed, more than 9 million savings accounts were wiped out, and 500,000 homeowners lost their homes to foreclosure. There was violence in the streets. Children were starving. Many Americans questioned the entire U.S. system of capitalism and democracy. The only hope left for most people was the upcoming 1932 presidential election. People wondered if there was a new leader who could save the country.

THE PRESIDENTIAL ELECTION OF 1932

At the Republican National Convention in the summer of 1932, President Hoover was re-nominated for a second term. It was a quiet convention; there were few accomplishments from the previous four years to celebrate. The

Roosevelt was an effective campaigner. During the 1932 campaign, he often stopped to speak personally to American voters, listening to their problems. *(Library of Congress)*

By 1933, about 25 percent of America's banks had closed and more than 9 million bank accounts were wiped out. These Bowery Savings Bank customers were frantically withdrawing their money. *(Library of Congress)*

Democrats had a more important decision to make. It was almost a certainty that whomever they nominated would become the next president. The country was more than ready for a change of leadership.

At the Democratic National Convention, there was a tight battle between the 1928 presidential candidate Alfred E. Smith and the new governor of New York, Franklin Delano Roosevelt. Roosevelt was the frontrunner, but he lacked the two-thirds majority of the delegates needed for nomination. The deadlock remained after three ballots. Before the fourth ballot, Roosevelt made a deal with the third candidate, Speaker of the House James Garner from Texas. In return for Garner's delegates, Roosevelt offered Garner the vice presidency. Garner's delegates were enough to give Roosevelt the nomination on the fourth ballot. At his acceptance speech the next day, Roosevelt told the delegates, "I pledge you, I pledge myself, to a new deal for the American people."

During the election, the phrase "New Deal" became Roosevelt's campaign slogan and "Happy Days Are Here Again" his campaign song. He advocated huge federal relief programs, the immediate repeal of Prohibition, public works projects, and a reduction in Hoover's protective tariffs. Hoover had little choice but to run on his record for the previous four years. The

When a foreclosed farm was put up for sale, farmers often held a penny auction to save it for the owner. At the auction to sell off the farmer's belongings, the other farmers bid only pennies and forbade any higher bids. They would then return the belongings to the farmer and apply the money raised to his mortgage.

When Roosevelt took office in 1933, he promised the American people action on the overwhelming problems of the depression. *(Library of Congress)*

election on November 8, 1932, was another landslide, this time for Roosevelt and the Democrats. FDR, as he came to be called during his presidency, carried 42 states and won the electoral college vote 472 to 59.

The period between the election and the inauguration of the president is called the interregnum. In 1932, the interregnum lasted nearly 4 months as Roosevelt was not due to take office until March 4, 1933. (In 1933, the Twentieth Amendment to the Constitution would reduce the interregnum to a little over two months setting the inauguration date at January 20.) The outgoing president is often called a lame duck because it is difficult for him to get legislation passed during this time. This was a particular problem during the interregnum between Hoover's term and Roosevelt's,

Babe Didrikson set world records at the 1932 Olympics in the javelin throw and the 80-meter hurdles. *(Library of Congress)*

On her flight across the Atlantic, Amelia Earhart was forced to land in a pasture of cows because of mechanical problems. *(Library of Congress)*

In 1932, athlete Babe Didrikson won two gold medals in track at the Olympic Games held in Los Angeles. She would later go on to become one of the greatest female golfers ever. In 1950, the Associated Press voted her the "greatest woman athlete" of the first half of the 20th century.

when one of the worst crises of the depression occurred. The nation's banking system broke down, and no one seemed to have the power to do anything about it.

As Americans became more and more protective of the money they had, banks experienced runs, in which depositors withdrew all their savings. But because banks had made bad investments, they did not have all their depositors' savings. The runs quickly bankrupted the banks, and many families' savings were wiped out. The only way to prevent the runs was for state governors to declare bank holidays and close the banks.

Nevada and Louisiana closed their banks soon after the 1932 election. In February 1933, Michigan and Maryland banks closed their doors. Before FDR was inaugurated on March 4, ten more states, including the crucial state of New York, declared bank holidays. When New York's banks closed, the New York Stock Exchange also shut down.

When Hoover was informed on inauguration morning that Illinois and New York had joined the list of states whose banks had closed, he said, "We are at the end of our string. There is nothing more we can do." But the nation had a new president who had not given up hope. At Roosevelt's inauguration the new president confidently told America, "The only thing we have to fear is fear itself." Millions of Americans waited anxiously to see if the "new deal" he promised them would work.

CHAPTER 3

ROOSEVELT'S FIRST NEW DEAL, 1933

Many Americans took to the roads, hitchhiking around the country to try to find work during the depression. No matter where they went, jobs were very scarce. *(Library of Congress)*

WHEN FRANKLIN D. ROOSEVELT assumed the presidency in March 1933, many people in America were suffering. Unemployment had reached 16 million, and the banking system had collapsed. Throughout his campaign, Roosevelt had made a connection with Americans; they believed he understood their problems. Roosevelt had been born into a rich family, but he had suffered a great tragedy in his life that helped him understand human suffering.

Young Franklin Roosevelt was an only child and grew up in a wealthy, loving family.
(Franklin D. Roosevelt Presidential Library and Museum)

In 1920, wheat sold for $3 a bushel; in 1932, it sold for 30¢ a bushel.

THE NEW PRESIDENT

Roosevelt was born on January 30, 1882, in Hyde Park, New York. As a child, he had the advantages of wealth. Up until the age of 14, he was taught by tutors. His family spent summer vacations in Europe or at their vacation home on Campobello Island in New Brunswick, Canada. Like his distant cousin and former president, Theodore "Teddy" Roosevelt, he developed a love of the outdoors, especially sports and natural history. At age 14, he was sent to a prestigious private academy, Groton School, in Massachusetts. One of Roosevelt's favorite teachers at Groton taught him that the wealthy in American society have an obligation to help the poor.

Roosevelt graduated from Harvard College in 1903 and showed a particular interest in history and politics. This interest led him to attend Columbia Law School, and he passed the New York State bar exam in 1907. After three years of practicing law, Roosevelt decided to enter politics and, at the age of 28, won his first election as a New York State senator. Like his cousin Teddy Roosevelt 20 years earlier, Franklin Roosevelt made a name for himself in state politics as an independent reformer, even defying the powerful and corrupt Tammany Hall politicians in New York City.

Roosevelt campaigned very hard for Woodrow Wilson's presidential election in 1912. When Wilson took office, he was rewarded with the post of assistant secretary of the navy, the same post Teddy Roosevelt had held. Franklin Roosevelt held the post until 1920 and helped develop the navy into the strong force that helped the United States win World War I. Roosevelt's experience and name made him a national figure. The Democrats tried to increase the appeal of their 1920 presidential ticket by nominating him for vice president to run with Ohio governor James Cox.

A war-weary country abandoned the Democrats and elected Ohio senator Warren G. Harding, who promised a "return to normalcy." It was Roosevelt's

first political defeat. A far greater tragedy would strike him the following year when he contracted polio, a disease that left him confined to a wheelchair or in leg braces for the rest of his life. Despite intense pain and nearly useless legs, Roosevelt returned to political life in New York, supporting Alfred E. Smith in his elections to New York governor in 1922 and 1926, and in Smith's two attempts to win the Democratic presidential nomination in 1924 and 1928. When Smith won the nomination in 1928, he convinced Roosevelt to run for his vacant New York State governor's post. Smith lost the presidency, but Roosevelt won the election for governor.

As governor, Roosevelt again became a national figure with his effective leadership of New York through the early years of the depression. He learned to get things done by developing support from different groups for his plans and working with the leaders of the

At Harvard College, Roosevelt (front row, center) served as editor of the prestigious school newspaper, *The Harvard Crimson*. *(Franklin D. Roosevelt Presidential Library and Museum)*

After serving in the Wilson administration, Roosevelt (right) was chosen to run for vice president in 1920. The presidential candidate was Ohio governor James Cox (left). *(Library of Congress)*

"I shall ask the Congress for broad executive power to wage war against the emergency, as great as the power that would be given to me if we were invaded by a foreign foe."

—President Roosevelt in his inauguration speech

opposing party. He also kept in touch with the people by speaking to them in his friendly, confident voice over the radio. By 1932, he was the Democrats' nominee for president, and he easily won the election over President Hoover. Millions of Americans looked to Roosevelt for the changes he promised, which the country so desperately needed.

THE FIRST HUNDRED DAYS

Roosevelt knew Americans did not want to hear any more promises of prosperity being just around the corner. They wanted action, and Roosevelt gave it to them. In his first one hundred days in office, 15 major laws were passed to deal with the country's problems. These new laws created a level of government intervention that the country had always resisted, but they probably saved the nation from economic collapse. Roosevelt concentrated on four major areas: farming, industry, direct relief to the poor and unemployed, and financial institutions.

The most critical problem was the banking system. As Hoover's term ended, banks throughout the country were shutting down, wiping out many Americans' life savings. The situation was so bad that many states declared bank holidays to prevent further damage. Roosevelt addressed the bank crisis immediately after his inauguration by calling Congress into special session and declaring a national bank holiday. Within a few days, Congress nearly unanimously passed Roosevelt's Emergency Banking Act on the same day he submitted it.

The act removed the United States from the gold standard and forbade the hoarding and export of gold. For years, the currencies of the world had been based on a set value of gold. Countries issued money according to the amount of gold they owned. (The United States stocks its gold reserves at Fort Knox, Kentucky.) This gold standard enabled countries with different currencies to trade with each other. By 1932, most nations, aside from the United States, had gone off the gold standard. Americans had been hoarding gold because they believed it was more valuable than U.S. currency. Because there was only a certain amount of gold in Fort Knox, more dollars could not be printed. As a result, money became scarce, and U.S. products became more expensive on the world market and harder to sell.

The Glass-Steagall Act required that all gold be turned in to a Federal Reserve bank, which would pay owners about $21 an ounce. This move gave the government control over the supply and value of the dollar. Money could now be issued to banks to meet their needs. However, banks could reopen only if they passed federal inspection. In addition, the federal government now had the power to supervise the banks' loan grants to make sure the bank's investments were sound. This act also created the Federal Deposit Insurance Corporation (FDIC), which guaranteed the first $5,000 that Americans deposited in their banks. Even if a bank failed, the government would return up to that amount to the depositor. The new laws restored faith in the banking system. Within weeks, Americans deposited more than a billion dollars back into their banks.

The Alphabet Agencies

Roosevelt was just beginning. In the first hundred days of his term, he established many laws and agencies to deal with specific problems in the country. Their long names were shortened to three or four letters and became known as the alphabet agencies. The first of these was the Civilian Conservation Corps, or CCC, which was both an employment and conservation program.

President Hoover (left) accompanied president-elect Roosevelt (right) to his 1933 inauguration. The two had become bitter rivals, and Hoover refused to speak to Roosevelt on the ride. *(Library of Congress)*

"He gave us back the banks and beer in one week. What more could the country ask? If the fellow didn't do another deed his whole time in the White House, I guess we'd have to be happy for that much."

—A Wisconsin citizen after FDR's first hundred days in office

About 3 million young men found work through the CCC during the 1930s. Right, dead wood is cleared from Sequoia National Park in California. *(Franklin D. Roosevelt Presidential Library and Museum)*

"If he burned down the capitol, we would all cheer and say, 'Well, we at least got a fire started anyhow.'"

—Humorist Will Rogers on the support Roosevelt received from Americans during his first months in office

As President Roosevelt's secretary of agriculture, Henry Wallace took drastic steps to raise farm prices. He later served as Roosevelt's vice president. *(Library of Congress)*

The CCC enrolled 250,000 men between the ages of 18 to 25 who came from families on relief. The young men received room and board and $30 a month, $25 of which was sent home to their families. The CCC worked on many different conservation projects, including improving national parks, draining marshes to control mosquitos and disease, building dams and roads, and planting 17 million new acres of forest.

Roosevelt addressed the plight of farmers with the Agricultural Adjustment Act (AAA). The most important aspect of the AAA was the federal government's control over production. The prices of farmers' goods could rise only if there was a balance between supply and demand. One reason farm prices had sunk so low was that many crops had been overproduced. The problem had started with World War I, when there was a world-wide demand for U.S. food.

The AAA, under the guidance of Secretary of Agriculture Henry Wallace, sent agents to every state to check on such commodities as grain, cotton, and live-stock. As a result of the agents' findings, a very painful decision had to be made. To raise farm prices to the point where American farmers could survive, many supplies had to be destroyed. Cotton had been so

The United States's gold reserves are stored at Fort Knox, Kentucky. The gold is kept in an underground chamber 60 feet long and 40 feet wide with walls 2 feet thick. *(Library of Congress)*

overproduced that cotton farmers had to plow under 10 million acres of cotton, one-third of the nation's crop. More than 6 million piglets were slaughtered, and millions of oranges were burned to reduce supply and raise prices. In return, the farmers received sorely needed relief payments. The AAA also allocated $2 billion to banks so that farmers could refinance their mortgages at lower rates of interest, allowing many farmers to repurchase their foreclosed lands.

An assassination attempt was made on the life of President Roosevelt in Miami, Florida, on February 15, 1933. Roosevelt escaped injury, but the mayor of Chicago, Anton Cermak, was killed by the assassin Giuseppe Zangara.

CCC laborers worked to conserve the country's natural resources. Left, CCC men work on a project in Beltsville, Maryland. *(Library of Congress)*

In 1933, a new Bonus Army of 3,000 men marched on Washington, D.C., to try to get their veterans' bonus payment. Roosevelt treated them much differently than President Hoover had a year earlier. He fed them, housed them in army barracks, and waived the CCC age requirement to get jobs for 2,600 of them.

It is estimated that more than 9 million bank accounts were wiped out by the banking crisis of the early 1930s.

THE HOBO JUNGLES

During the depression, many migratory workers came to be known as hoboes. Most looked for work, but during the hard times, jobs were scarce. Their poverty forced many of them to live outside towns in communities that were usually near the rail lines. Their shelters were built of whatever stray materials that they could find, and their meals were sometimes called Mulligan stews, consisting of whatever food they could scrounge.

These communities were known as hobo jungles because the drifters tried to hide in the tall grass and weeds away from the tracks. Like most communities, a code of rules developed among the hoboes. The worst crime was jackrolling, or stealing, and was punished with beatings and exile. Besides their poverty, hoboes shared the common dangers of jumping trains and beatings from railroad detectives.

The jungles were full of hoboes who had lost a leg or an arm from train injuries. They were also full of America's minorities. African Americans, Latinos, and American Indians, as well as whites, often lived together sharing food, water, and information about jobs. The hobo jungle was one place in America where racial equality was usually not a big problem.

The Tennessee Valley Authority (TVA) was one of Roosevelt's most successful programs, again combining both employment and conservation. The Tennessee River valley includes areas of seven states: Tennessee, Alabama, Kentucky, North Carolina, Mississippi, Georgia, and Virginia. Before the TVA project, this area was one of the country's poorest rural regions. The Tennessee River often flooded, bringing destruction to the homes and crops of those who lived in the valley.

The TVA hired 40,000 men to build a series of dams and power stations to control the river and bring cheap electricity to the area's inhabitants, mostly farmers. The project also helped restore the fertility of the farmland and prevent soil erosion. Electricity brought farmers improved technology to make farming easier while enabling families in the area to have refrigeration, radio, and improved sanitation, vastly improving their lives and increasing consumer demand for goods. Once the project was completed, youth from the CCC helped rebuild the valley land

TVA workers, such as the man at left, made huge improvements in navigation, flood control, and electricity availability for thousands of residents of the Tennessee Valley. *(Library of Congress)*

The average U.S. salary during the 1930s was $1,368 per year. Milk cost 14¢ a quart, bread cost 9¢ a loaf, and steak cost 42¢ a pound.

by planting trees and teaching farmers soil conservation. As a result of the TVA, cash from farming in the Tennessee River valley rose 200 percent.

With the Federal Emergency Relief Act (FERA), Roosevelt did what Hoover had found impossible—he gave direct relief to Americans most in need. In early 1933, 6 million Americans were on city and state relief and 15 million were out of work. FERA, under the guidance of Roosevelt's close assistant and adviser Harry Hopkins, allocated $500 million in direct cash payments for these people.

FERA helped alleviate much suffering at the height of the depression, but Roosevelt looked upon it as a temporary measure. By the end of the year, the Civil Works Administration (CWA) was created within FERA, which turned the focus from relief to employment. The CWA provided work for up to 4 million people in

Construction of new houses fell 95 percent from 1928 to 1933.

The reservoir created by Hoover Dam, Lake Mead, covers 233 square miles. *(Library of Congress)*

President Roosevelt's supporters ordered that the name of the Hoover Dam be changed to the Boulder Dam during his presidency. President Truman changed it back to the Hoover Dam in 1947.

construction, social work, and the teaching of literacy. CWA workers built 240,000 miles of roads, 5,000 public buildings, and hundreds of new airports.

Just as the AAA had helped farmers recover their lost land, Roosevelt set up the Home Owners' Loan Corporation (HOLC) to help Americans who had lost their homes, some as far back as 1930. Under this program, the mortgage holder (usually a bank) of a foreclosed home could turn it over to the government in return for a guaranteed government bond. The government would then return the homes to their owners and refinance their mortgage at a low rate The HOLC eventually helped 1 million families keep homes that they would have lost or had already lost without the program.

All of these programs were very successful at helping to solve the most severe problems of the depression, but some programs had mixed results. One of these was the National Recovery Administration (NRA), which Roosevelt considered his most far-reaching program. The

THE EYES AND EARS OF THE PRESIDENT

Few first ladies have played as important a role in their husband's presidency as Eleanor Roosevelt did. She began to work politically for FDR in the 1920s after polio limited his ability to move around. As president, FDR referred to his wife as his "eyes and ears" because she would make fact-finding trips for him to help him make important decisions. She also had strong opinions on such issues as women's rights, desegregation, and youth employment, and she became an influential figure during FDR's presidency.

Eleanor Roosevelt was a niece of Teddy Roosevelt and a distant cousin of her husband. During the depression, she traveled all over the nation on lecture tours and wrote a daily newspaper column on issues of the time. During the depression, she sponsored an experiment in West Virginia to create a self-sustaining community for poor coal miners and their families.

Her most famous political stand came in 1939 when she resigned from the Daughters of the American Revolution (DAR) over the issue of racial inequality. The DAR had refused to allow the famed African-American singer Marian Anderson to sing at Constitution Hall in Washington, D.C., because of her race. Eleanor Roosevelt arranged instead for Anderson to sing before 75,000 people at the Lincoln Memorial.

More than twice as much concrete was poured during the TVA project than was used in the building of the Panama Canal.

TVA dams like the one under construction below in Tennessee controlled flooding and produced electricity. *(Library of Congress)*

One month after Roosevelt's first hundred days, the German Reichstag declared the National Socialist Party, the Nazis, to be Germany's only political party.

NRA tried to encourage cooperation between labor and management. Roosevelt believed that it would be good for the economy to allow large corporations to work together to set standards for production and prices. As a result, the NRA suspended the antitrust laws though the government kept the authority to regulate these standards. Businesses were also required to establish codes on competition and fair labor standards. However, the government only licensed businesses that agreed to a minimum wage and limited work hours. Workers also gained the right to choose their own unions and organize for collective bargaining. Union busting, or the forced break-up of unions, was outlawed.

The NRA eventually collapsed under its own weight, drafting more than 700 codes regulating various industries. Some businesspeople renamed the NRA the National Run Around as the codes wound up restricting business more than encouraging it. For example, one code forbade industries from making technological advances if it led to layoffs of workers. The NRA also tried to limit child labor by establishing a minimum age of 16 for employment in most industries and 18 for more dangerous jobs. However, the limitation only lasted for two years because the Supreme Court later ruled the law unconstitutional.

Roosevelt tackled America's huge unemployment problem with the formation of the Public Works Administration (PWA). Congress gave this program a budget of $3.3 billion to fund construction projects across the nation. Between 1933 and 1939, more than one million Americans found work through the PWA, which completed more than 35,000 projects, including the construction of highways, hospitals, bridges, dams, universities, and waterworks. The PWA also built more than 20,000 units of low-cost housing, which charged only $26 a month for rent. In the big cities, PWA workers tore down the worst slums and built affordable apartment buildings.

OTHER PROGRAMS

There were several other noteworthy accomplishments made by Roosevelt and his cooperative Congress during the first hundred days. The Securities Act tried to prevent the stock fraud that had contributed to the stock market crash of 1929 by requiring brokers to provide complete information about the stocks they sold. One year later, the Securities and Exchange Commision (SEC) was created to regulate the New York Stock Exchange by licensing all stocks traded and forbidding the sale of stocks on margin.

The Wagner-Peyser Act created the United States Employment Service and provided funds to states to set up their own local employment offices. To help balance the federal budget, the Economy Act cut $500 million from veterans' payments and federal employees' wages. At Roosevelt's urging, Congress also passed an amendment to the Volstead Act, which had prohibited the sale of alcohol. Under the new law, beer containing 3.2 percent alcohol could now be sold legally. It was the

Between 1933 and 1943, the PWA spent more than $4 billion on public projects. The project above was the building of a dam on the Mississippi River. *(Franklin D. Roosevelt Presidential Library and Museum)*

"You feel like charging Hell with a bucket of water."

—Future president Lyndon B. Johnson in 1933 when he first came to Washington to work for the New Deal

FDR named New York state industrial commissioner Frances Perkins as secretary of labor, making her the first woman to be appointed a cabinet member.

"Let's concentrate on one thing: save the people and the nation and if we have to change our minds twice every day to accomplish that end, we should do it."

—President Roosevelt to his cabinet soon after taking office

beginning of the end of Prohibition. The Twenty-first Amendment to the Constitution, which repealed Prohibition would be passed by the end of 1933.

FIRESIDE CHATS AND THE RISE OF RADIO

The late 1920s and early 1930s saw a tremendous rise in the popularity of radio in America. The first local stations started broadcasting in 1920, and the first national network, the National Broadcasting Company (NBC), was formed in 1926. When Roosevelt took office in 1933, more than half of the country's 30 million homes owned at least one radio. Those who did not own a radio were listening, too, either at friends' homes or in Main Street businesses.

Roosevelt understood the importance of radio in transmitting information and took advantage of the

President Roosevelt delivers one of his fireside chats on radio. He was the first president to use the media to appeal directly to the public. *(AP/Wide World)*

new medium. Just one week after taking office, Roosevelt broadcast his first fireside chat to explain to Americans that their banks would be reopening the next day. Over the next 12 years, Roosevelt would give about 30 of these fireside chats to explain his policies to the American people and enlist their support. The broadcasts contributed greatly to Roosevelt's popularity as his friendly, persuasive voice reassured millions that the country was overcoming the problems of the depression.

Roosevelt also used the press conference as no other president had before. Twice a week, he allowed reporters to come into the White House for open discussions, and he even asked for their opinions. The result was tremendous press coverage and support among the nation's important newspapers and, therefore, their readers.

Roosevelt's fireside chats were just one example of how radio provided Americans with important information instantly. Radio news programs could provide news much faster than newspapers and to a national audience. News became vitally important to Americans in the 1930s as Roosevelt's New Deal programs fought the depression and as war winds blew once again in Europe. Thanks to radio, sports fans could hear their events live instead of having to wait for their local newspaper's account a day or two later. As Americans became more and more hooked on news, radio stations hired their own reporters and commentators to explain the news to their listeners.

Radio's greatest strength, however, was providing free entertainment to Americans who needed escape from the fears of everyday life in the depression. Radio brought music into American homes and helped popularize new styles, such as swing and crooning. Crooners such as Bing Crosby used of the radio microphone and developed a softer, more personal style of singing. Swing was a more structured form of jazz that became popular among both whites and African Americans later in the decade as they danced to its strong beat.

"Without bloodshed, the New Deal defanged our most dangerous internal crisis since the crisis of 1861 [the Civil War]."

—New Deal official Thomas Corcoran on Roosevelt's New Deal

As secretary of labor, Frances Perkins defended the rights of workers and supported child welfare legislation. *(Library of Congress)*

"Radio has given the president a weapon such as no ruler has ever known."

—The editor of *Radio Guide* in a 1934 editorial

Marian Anderson was the first African American to perform at the Metropolitan Opera House in New York. *(Library of Congress)*

The sitcom, or situation comedy, which is so popular on television today, had its roots in radio. The most popular of these radio comedies was *Amos 'n' Andy,* a show performed by white actors using an exaggerated African-American dialect to portray the antics of several African-American characters. The NAACP complained that the show was insulting to African Americans, but 30 million Americans, including many African Americans, listened devotedly to each show, which aired for 15 minutes Monday through Friday. Movie theaters would even interrupt their movies to broadcast *Amos 'n' Andy* to their customers.

Radio pleased almost everyone by offering many different kinds of shows. Today's television soap opera, revealing the personal lives of everyday characters, also had its beginnings on radio. Shows such as *The Guiding Light, Days of Our Lives,* and *As the World Turns* amazingly have survived from their beginnings on radio to the 21st century on television. Soap operas received their name from their original radio sponsors, which were usually soap manufacturers.

As Congress adjourned on June 16, 1933, the first hundred days of amazing legislative activity gave most Americans hope. The immediate results of the New Deal included the rescue of the banking system, the employment of many more Americans, and direct relief to many of the neediest. It was still too early to judge the New Deal completely, but Americans were relieved that the president was at least trying. The real test would be in the coming months and years.

CHAPTER 4

SETBACKS AND OPPOSITION, 1934–1935

R OOSEVELT'S NEW DEAL PROGRAMS resulted in immediate gains in employment, hunger relief, the rescue of homes and farms from foreclosure, and a stable banking system. However, by 1934, there were still 10 million Americans unemployed, and the U.S. economy was still weak. Part of the problem was a worldwide economic depression, but another part was the failure of the NRA program to stimulate the American economy. As industrial production continued to decline and the NRA codes hindered business, voices of opposition were heard in America. In 1933, Roosevelt had the support of nearly every sector of America, but by 1934, the honeymoon was over.

Labor unrest grew significantly during the depression. Strikes, like the one by laundry workers above, affected millions of workers. *(Library of Congress)*

"Roosevelt's programs aren't any more useful than a jar of warm spit."

—Senator Huey Long of Louisiana

Senator Huey Long became one of President Roosevelt's most outspoken opponents. Long opposed much of Roosevelt's New Deal for not doing enough to end poverty. *(Library of Congress)*

After one radio broadcast in 1931, Father Coughlin received over 1 million letters of approval. As his views became more extreme, the Catholic Church ordered him off the air. *(Library of Congress)*

Big business was the first to voice opposition. In August 1934, businessleaders, lawyers, and prominent politicians, including Roosevelt's ex-ally Alfred Smith, formed the American Liberty League. The members of this group condemned Roosevelt's programs as tyrannical and socialistic. (Socialism is an economic system in which the government controls industrial production.) They particularly hated the NRA because they believed it was granting labor far too many benefits and was hurting business. As Roosevelt pushed new taxes on the wealthy to pay for his New Deal programs, the wealthy joined the opposition.

VOICES OF OPPOSITION

Several of Roosevelt's opponents rose to national fame in 1934. Some people said he was doing too much, some said he was not doing enough, and some considered a presidential run against him in the 1936 election. The most outspoken was Democratic senator Huey Long of Louisiana whose slogan was "Every man a king." Long had supported Roosevelt in 1932 but thought the president had not done enough to alleviate the poverty in America.

Long was outraged that there were so many multimillionaires in America while millions lived in poverty. He proposed a Share Our Wealth program in which one-third of the nation's money would be divided among all the people. Long also wanted to limit personal fortunes to about $3 million. Fortunes in excess of this amount would be used to provide free homesteads, free education, free cars, and a guaranteed income of $2,000 a year for every American. Most economists of the day said Long's program was ridiculous, but Long's supporters pointed out what the senator had accomplished in Louisiana. In just six years as governor and senator, Long had greatly improved Louisiana's roads, schools, and hospitals.

Long was considered a very strong opponent of Roosevelt for the 1936 Democratic nomination for president, but the senator had many enemies in Louisiana due to his ruthless methods. He hired and fired all officeholders in the state and had handpicked his successor as governor to carry out his programs. Long had been impeached while governor by the Louisiana House of Representatives for bribery and misuse of state funds, but he was later acquitted by the state senate. In 1935, he was assassinated in Baton Rouge, Louisiana, by a longtime political opponent.

Just as President Roosevelt used radio to inform the public of his policies, his critics also used it to publicize their opposition. A Catholic priest, Father Charles Coughlin, had a national weekly program called *The Golden Hour of the Little Flower.* Coughlin had a huge audience estimated at 30 to 40 million listeners. He was a strong Roosevelt supporter at first, calling the New Deal "Christ's Deal."

By late 1934, Coughlin's disappointment in the New Deal led him to abandon Roosevelt and capitalism. He said the president had turned the nation over to "international bankers," and he embraced socialism, calling for the government to take over industry and employ everyone. Coughlin formed his own political party, the National Union for Social Justice, which picked North Dakota congressman William Lemke as its presidential candidate in 1936. By that time, however, Coughlin's speech had grown more and more extreme. He was an anti-Semite (a person who discriminates against Jews), who blamed wealthy Jewish bankers for corrupting the New Deal. He even preached about the need for America to have a dictator like Nazi Germany's Adolf Hitler. Coughlin's popularity dropped quickly, and Lemke was not a factor in the 1936 election.

End Poverty in California (EPIC) was another movement whose members thought Roosevelt had not done enough. EPIC had been founded by writer Upton

"I'm a small fish here in Washington, but I'm the Kingfish to the folks down in Louisiana."

—Louisiana senator Huey Long explaining his nickname of Kingfish

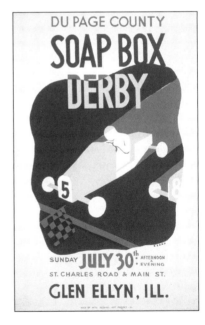

The first Soap Box Derby was held in Dayton, Ohio, in 1934. The winner, Bob Turner of Muncie, Indiana, built his racer from laminated wood taken from a saloon bar. *(Library of Congress)*

WANTED: DEAD OR ALIVE

The hard times of the depression led to a marked increase in crime, particularly bank robberies. Just as in the old West, some of these outlaws became heroes to many Americans. One reason was that the banks, which were responsible for so many foreclosures of people's homes and farms, were looked upon as the enemy, especially in the Midwest. Newspapers of the day also sensationalized the exploits of the robbers to attract readers.

The most famous of the bank robbers was probably John Dillinger, who often made daring escapes whenever he was captured by the police. He gained a reputation as a Robin Hood among thieves because he once gave carfare home to a couple of his hostages after an escape. He murdered 10 men in his career until he was finally gunned down by FBI agents outside a Chicago movie theater. Dillinger was the FBI's first "Public Enemy Number One."

Bonnie Parker and Clyde Barrow, or Bonnie and Clyde, became famous for a two-year robbery and murder spree throughout Missouri, Texas, New Mexico, and Oklahoma. Bonnie and Clyde became known for their car chases with the police and the many photos they took of themselves posing with their weapons. The photos eventually helped the police track down the flamboyant couple. The police shot and killed Bonnie and Clyde in a roadblock ambush.

Many of the outlaws had colorful nicknames, such as Pretty Boy Floyd, Baby Face Nelson, Machine Gun Kelly, and Ma Barker, who taught all four of her sons how to be bank robbers.

Bonnie and Clyde killed 12 people during their crime spree throughout the Southwest in 1932–34. *(AP/Wide World)*

Soap box derbies became very popular during the 1930s. One competition drew 40,000 spectators.

Sinclair, who had written the influential muckraking novel *The Jungle* in 1906 exposing the unsanitary working conditions in the meat industry. The novel led to America's first pure food and drug laws, passed during Teddy Roosevelt's presidency, and started Sinclair's career as a socialist politician.

Sinclair's EPIC program called on government to purchase all unused land and hire the unemployed to grow their own food on it. Under the program, the government would also purchase unused factories where the unemployed could make many of their own goods. Sinclair called for much higher taxes on the wealthy and a $50 a month pension for all Americans over age 60. He won the Democratic nomination to run for governor of California in 1934, but the state's wealthy, especially those in the movie business, campaigned hard against him, and he was defeated.

Another California reformer whose plan for the elderly attracted national attention was Dr. Francis Townsend. His program was called the Old Age Revolving Pension, and Townsend believed it would solve the unemployment problem and benefit the elderly. Under the program, the government would remove all those over age 60 from the labor force and provide them a $200 pension every month. The pensioners would be required to spend the money each month, thus stimulating the economy and creating more jobs.

Townsend clubs started appearing throughout the country to support the idea, eventually totalling 7,000 groups with 3.5 million members. The program was introduced in Congress in 1935, where economists pointed out its flaws. Townsend planned to raise money for the program with a 2 percent national sales tax, which would hurt Americans at a time when they already could not afford to buy most things. Also, as a national program, the Townsend Plan would cost about $24 billion, much more than the sales tax would raise. The program was defeated, but Roosevelt was working on his own pension plan for America's elderly.

LABOR UPRISINGS

Roosevelt's NRA program resulted in some gains for labor in wages and shorter workweeks, but management still refused to cooperate with unions. As a result of this resistance and high unemployment, union

President Roosevelt originally supported Upton Sinclair, but as attacks labeled Sinclair a socialist, Roosevelt backed away. *(Library of Congress)*

"I have pleaded (labor's) case, not in the quavering tones of a feeble mendicant asking alms but in the thundering voice of the captain of a mighty host demanding the rights to which free men are entitled."

—United Mine Owners union leader John L. Lewis

Farmers often paid more to produce their goods than they could sell them for. Above, workers dump their milk rather than let it be sold at an unfair price. *(Library of Congress)*

membership fell from 5 million at the end of the 1920s to 2 million in 1933. The depression made workers realize more than ever that they needed their unions in order to have any power in the workplace.

Management also used the conditions of the depression to justify their refusal to allow workers to unionize. Businesses avoided the NRA law that allowed workers to unionize by forming company unions. Employers then only hired workers who agreed to join the company union. When workers still attempted to organize their own union, management hired spies to report on worker activities and armed guards to intimidate them. Tension between labor and management was ready to boil over.

In 1934, there were more than 1,800 strikes in America, affecting nearly 1.5 million workers. Many of

DANCE MARATHONS

One of the strangest forms of entertainment during the depression was the dance marathon. Most couples who entered the contests were desperate for the large cash prizes awarded to the winners, but some were professionals who were paid by promoters to keep audiences interested. Spectators paid a quarter to watch, and over the weeks or months that the marathon lasted, they rooted for their favorite couples.

The rules of the dance marathon were brutal. Couples danced to both fast and slow music for an hour and then got about a ten-minute rest. Loud sirens signalled the end of the break, and couples returned for another hour of dancing. The cycle went on 24 hours a day, week after week, as weary couples dragged each other over the dance floor. Many dancers had to be treated for exhaustion, and some deaths were even reported, but audiences flocked to the marathons to see who would be the last couple left standing.

The marathons were presented in a theatrical way to keep audiences involved. If interest was fading, promoters often staged something spectacular, like a sprint. During a sprint, the exhausted couples were tied to each other and forced to run around the dance floor until several couples were eliminated by collapsing. Sometimes fake deaths were staged to get the audience involved again. Some of the professional couples had acts they performed, and they were rewarded with coins from their fans. A famous book titled *They Shoot Horses, Don't They?* was written by Horace McCoy about the dance marathons of the depression. It was later made into a movie.

Dance marathons were eventually banned in most areas due to the risks to the dancers' lives. *(Granger Collection)*

these work stoppages turned violent. In Minneapolis, the Brotherhood of Teamsters (truck drivers) union staged a strike that crippled the city's transportation system. The Teamsters' employers had formed a group called the Citizens' Alliance, and they refused to acknowledge the union. The Alliance also formed a Citizen's Army to oppose the strikers. Over the next three months, there were several violent battles between the two sides, resulting in four deaths and many more injured. When a general strike of the city's workers started, the governor of Minnesota declared martial law and persuaded management to accept the Teamsters' union.

In San Francisco, employers refused to recognize the longshoremen's (dockworkers) union, the workers

The biggest issue for strikers during the 1930s was their right to have a union. Below, striking miners in West Virginia line up for food rations. *(Library of Congress)*

struck and closed down the docks. On July 5, the police were sent in to try to reopen the docks. Violence broke out, leaving two strikers dead and many others wounded. The National Guard had to be called in to restore order. The Teamsters and other unions soon went out on strike in support of the longshoremen in a general strike that nearly shut down the city. The strike ended when the longshoremen accepted arbitration. (In this process, a judge, or other other objective expert, settles the dispute.) The arbitration for the longshoremen eventually gained them their union and wage increases.

In the South, seven textile workers were killed when their company hired armed strikebreakers to oppose them. The workers eventually won their demands when textile workers from across the country also went out on strike in solidarity. In Milwaukee, striking streetcar workers destroyed dozens of streetcars. In Philadelphia, cabdrivers burned a hundred taxis. In the strike on the United Mine Owners in Pennsylvania, company henchmen set crosses on fire and bombed miners' homes. Big strikebreaking firms made millions of dollars as companies hired their armies of men to come in with guns, nightsticks, and tear gas to break the strikers. It was becoming clear the NRA was not strong enough to get workers their unions.

COMMUNISTS AND LABOR

During the many strikes of the mid-1930s, management often accused union leaders of being communist, or Red. (In the 1930s, communists supported the idea of an economic system in which a worker-controlled government, rather than private individuals, owned everything and managed the production, distribution, and use of all goods and labor.) Management's intent was to gain public support for their strikebreaking tactics and avoid negotiations with the leaders. It is true that some strike organizers were members of the

Eager for inexpensive entertainment during the depression, Americans turned to the new craze of the jigsaw puzzle, buying more than 4 million in 1934 alone. Said one fan, "It's one problem I can solve."

A shorter work week was another issue workers and management fought over. Here, female employees at Woolworth's in New York City strike for a 40-hour work week. *(Library of Congress)*

Communist Party. The party's belief that government should control industry was very appealing to a workforce that capitalism (the system of private ownership and free, uncontrolled markets) was currently failing to support. As a result, membership in the party grew during the mid-1930s. Communist Party members played a prominent role in many strikes, including the Ford autoworkers strike in Michigan in 1932, during which four demonstrators were killed, and the San Francisco general strike in 1934.

Strikes in the 1930s often turned violent as workers and management clashed. Management sometimes hired thugs to start the violence so they could blame it on the workers. *(Illustrated London News Picture Library)*

America's first parking meters went into service in Oklahoma City, Oklahoma, in 1935. The meters cut down on traffic and raised money for the city government. Cars park along the "new" parking meters in Omaha, Nebraska, in 1938. *(Library of Congress)*

Management pointed to the violence of these strikes to create a Red Scare around the country and disrupt union activity. There were even incidents in which strikebreakers staged a random bombing or other violence to blame on the Reds. The tactic excited many Americans' patriotism and resulted in some opposition to the workers' demands. However, it became clear to most Americans that the labor union was the only aspect of communism in which the workers were interested. The ultimate goal of the Communist Party, the overthrow of capitalism in America, was not the purpose of most workers who were seeking bargaining power with their employers.

DUST BOWL DROUGHT DEEPENS

In 1934 and early 1935, nature itself seemed to be acting against Roosevelt and his New Deal programs. The drought that had started in the Midwest in 1930

"I will say one thing for this administration. It's the one time when the fellow with money is worrying more than the one without it."

—American humorist Will Rogers

A dust storm, or black blizzard, rolls in on a small midwestern town. There was usually little warning that a storm was coming. *(National Archives)*

Auto repair shops did excellent business during the depression as people had to repair their old cars rather than buy new ones.

Chicago, Illinois, hosted a World's Fair in 1933–34 celebrating the one hundredth anniversary of the city. The fair attracted nearly 40 million visitors. *(Library of Congress)*

became the worst in American history, affecting 27 states severely. Dust storms increased from 14 in 1932 to 40 in 1935. The *Yearbook for Agriculture* for 1934 announced that 35 million acres of farmland had been destroyed and another 100 million acres had little, if any, topsoil left. During the summer of 1934, the temperature rose above 100 degrees Fahrenheit for 36 consecutive days in Oklahoma. The Great Plains, where crops had once flourished, turned into a desert.

Occasional drought was part of the Midwest's weather cycle, but in previous cycles, the tall grasses had kept the soil intact. The grasses had disappeared from years of overcultivation and overgrazing, and without the tight network of the grasses' roots to hold it in place, the topsoil blew away. When the winds picked up, this resulted in dust storms called black blizzards, which were miles wide, reached several thousand feet high, and came without warning.

The worst of the black blizzards hit the Texas and Oklahoma panhandles on Black Sunday, April 14, 1935. Winds of 60 miles an hour drove a huge black wall of dirt and debris over the area, turning day into night. It buried tractors in sand dunes, suffocated and killed livestock, and destroyed what little fertile land was

LIVING IN THE DUST BOWL

Surviving the dust storms that plagued the dust bowl states in the 1930s was just part of the battle. Even when there were no storms, the dust made everyday life a struggle. In addition to the usual chores, there were now the dust chores.

During the night, there was often enough wind to blow a drift of dust halfway up the front door. To get out of the house, it was necessary to climb out a window and shovel the dust away. Inside the house, bed-sheets were hung from the ceiling of each room to catch floating dust in the air. Before breakfast could be made, all the cooking utensils had to be cleaned of the dust that had settled on them. Clothes and bed-sheets had to be washed everyday to remove the dust from them. This task was difficult because farms did not have washing machines; each piece had to be washed by hand.

If there were babies in the family, their cribs had to be constantly covered with sheets to keep the infants from breathing in the dust and possibly suffocating to death. Older children and adults often slept with damp rags over their mouths to try to protect themselves. If a fire was needed at night to keep warm, the only fuel available to many families was cow chips (dried manure). They could not afford coal, and because the land had been cleared of trees long ago, the amount of wood was limited. It is not surprising that more than 2 million people left their homes in the dust bowl for a very uncertain future out West.

During the 1930s, approximately 2.5 million people moved out of the Midwest to escape the dust bowl. This was the largest migration in U.S. history.

Life in the dust bowl was hard to bear. Children slept with rags over their mouths to keep from breathing in dust, and it was often impossible to stay clean. *(Library of Congress)*

"Americans have been the greatest destroyers of land of any race or people, barbaric or civilized."

—Hugh Hammond Bennett, adviser to the Roosevelt administration on soil conservation

"This is the dust storm country. It is the saddest land I have ever seen."

—Reporter Ernie Pyle covering the dust bowl in Kansas

The get-rich-quick scheme of the chain letter started in 1935. Few people made much money from the scheme, but the U.S. Post Office had to hire extra help to deal with the millions of chain letters in the mail.

left. The blizzard was so strong that it generated its own electrical field, much as lightning is created during a thunderstorm, knocking out cars that tried to escape it. The storm blew all the way to Washington, D.C., by the next morning.

SUPREME COURT OPPOSITION

During Roosevelt's first term, the nine-member Supreme Court included four conservative judges who believed that government should not interfere in the business affairs of the nation. It also had three liberal justices who, like Roosevelt, believed the government had an obligation to intervene when necessary. They also supported New Deal programs. The remaining three members, called centrists, sometimes supported Roosevelt and sometimes did not. In 1935, when cases challenging the legality of several New Deal programs started reaching the Supreme Court, the judges became Roosevelt's biggest obstacle of all.

Supreme Court decisions struck down the NRA and the AAA, two of Roosevelt's most important New Deal programs. The NRA was declared unconstitutional in *Schechter Poultry Corporation v. United States.* The judges ruled that the NRA had intervened in a situation in which only the state had legal power. They supported their decision with the commerce clause of the Constitution, which gave Congress the right to regulate commerce with foreign nations and among states, but not within a single state. The decision was ominous for Roosevelt because most New Deal programs were regulating some aspect of state business as they provided assistance to various groups.

In January 1936, the court also declared Roosevelt's AAA program aiding farmers unconstitutional. In the *United States v. Butler,* the court determined that an AAA tax on processors who purchased farmers' goods was unconstitutional. The tax was intended to help farmers and had helped raise farmers' incomes 60 percent since the program began, but the judges decided it was an illegal use of the government's right to impose taxes. The government had to return $200 million in taxes to the processors. Its authority to control crop production and prices had ended.

Several other decisions, usually by a 5–4 vote, overturned other New Deal programs. The court decided the government had to redeem government bonds in gold instead of the paper currency Roosevelt had established. The court again used the commerce clause to overturn the Railroad Retirement Act, which mandated a pension to railroad workers.

Despite this opposition, Roosevelt believed he still had the support of the American people. He had promised them to be a president of action, dedicated to trying everything possible to overcome the horrible effects of the depression. He would not sit back and watch his New Deal being dismantled. He was already planning the second New Deal.

EUROPE SIMMERS AGAIN

In January 1933, just five weeks before President Roosevelt took office, Adolf Hitler was named chancellor of Germany by President Paul von Hindenburg. Hitler's Nazi Party had only received one third of the vote in the recent elections, but there were strong anticommunist feelings in Germany and Hitler was an arch anticommunist. Hindenberg's choice would change world history.

Hitler moved very quickly during 1933-34 to expand his power. In his rise, he was ruthless and took advantage of a German people who had been enduring a horrible depression since the Treaty of Versailles after World War I. In February 1933, Hitler suspended all civil liberties after the burning of the Reichstag government building. A Dutch Communist was convicted of the crime, but some believed the Nazis did it themselves as a ploy to create chaos and

The chief justice who overturned some of Roosevelt's New Deal programs was Charles Evans Hughes. Hughes was nearly elected president of the United States in 1916, but he had lost to Woodrow Wilson in a close election.

The German Reichstag was built in the late 19th century. It was destroyed by fire in 1933 and bombing during World War II (1939–45) but renovated in the 1990s. *(Library of Congress)*

A poster from ca. 1933 shows Germany's leaders von Hindenburg and Hitler. The words translate, "The Reich will never be destroyed when you stay united and loyal." *(Library of Congress)*

increase their influence. In March, Hitler called for new elections. The Nazis won control of the government, and Hitler gained the authority to decree laws.

In April 1933, Hitler dismissed all Jewish office-holders and mandated a boycott of Jewish business. When mobs attacked Jews and their shops throughout Germany, local authorities did nothing. In May, Hitler outlawed unions and had union leaders sent to work prisons called concentration camps. By the end of the year, he made the Nazi Party the only legal political party in the country and withdrew Germany from the League of Nations. In violation of the Treaty of Versailles, he also began a massive rebuilding of the German military.

On June 30, 1934, known as the Night of the Long Knives (a phrase from a popular Nazi song), Hitler had nearly 200 opponents within the Nazi Party murdered and said it was "in self-defense of the state." In August, when von Hindenburg died, Hitler assumed the presidency. He was now the absolute dictator of Germany and his plans went much further than that.

CHAPTER 5

THE SECOND NEW DEAL AND RE-ELECTION, 1935–1936

DESPITE THE SETBACKS ROOSEVELT suffered in the middle of his first term, there was one hopeful sign for him. In the 1934 congressional elections, the voters gave his Democratic Party huge increases in the party's majority in each house of Congress. In the House, 13 newly elected members of congress were Democrats, giving them a 322–103 majority. The gain in the Senate was nine senators, giving the Democrats a 69–31 edge. The clear message was that Roosevelt was still very popular with the people, and he had even more support than before to carry out more New Deal legislation.

Labor and management remained at odds throughout the 1930s. Sit-down strikes, like this one by auto workers in Flint, Michigan, which began in 1936, became an effective tactic for workers. *(Library of Congress)*

WORKS PROGRESS
ADMINISTRATION
P R E S E N T S

AN EXHIBITION
OF SELECTED SKILLS
OF THE UNEMPLOYED
JUNE 1 – JUNE 18
KAUFMANN'S
DEPARTMENT STORE
DIV OF WOMEN'S & PROFESSIONAL PROJECTS

The WPA included projects for those with special skills like teachers and artists. This poster announces a WPA arts and crafts exhibit in New York.
(Library of Congress)

"Artists got to eat just like other people."

—WPA director Harry Hopkins justifying the Federal One projects' hiring of writers, artists, musicians, and actors

In April 1935, with this added support in Congress, Roosevelt started to create a series of new programs starting that are usually called the second New Deal. The first of these was the Emergency Relief Appropriation Act, which provided nearly $5 billion to create more than 3 million jobs through public works projects. The Works Progress Administration (WPA) was set up to administer the program. It became the largest work relief program in U.S. history.

The pay for WPA jobs was low—$60 to $100 a month—because Roosevelt did not want the WPA to compete with private business. Roosevelt also wanted WPA projects to stimulate the economy, so that the money would circulate and return to the national treasury. Most of the jobs were in construction, and they included a wide range of projects. New schools, hospitals, and post offices were built and old ones repaired. Roads, especially in rural America, were improved or constructed anew. WPA workers also built bridges and airports. Recreation was emphasized as workers made playgrounds, parks, athletic fields, tennis courts, and swimming pools.

The WPA also set up the National Youth Administration (NYA) to help keep high school and college students in school. The students were paid up to $30 a month for jobs in their schools, where they worked as library clerks, tutors, and typists. Besides encouraging students to stay in school, the program kept them out of the labor force and eased the still-high unemployment numbers.

Because the purpose of the WPA was to provide employment and wages, mechanical power was avoided in favor of human labor to ensure the greatest number of workers. Over the next three years, the WPA created around 250,000 projects. The projects provided work for more than 5 million Americans and contributed more than $10 billion to the U.S. economy. By 1936, the WPA employed one-third of the nation's unemployed.

THE WPA SUPPORTS ARTISTS

The WPA with its Federal One projects was also the first agency in U.S. history to support the arts. These projects provided work for artists in the visual arts, theater, literature, and music. The arts projects were small, but they supported some of the most famous artists in each field and led to the creation of works that survive to this day. For example, artists in the Federal Art Project (FAP) created 2,500 murals and 18,000 sculptures for public buildings. It employed more than 9,000 workers, many of them teachers who taught art at community centers. Many artists in the FAP, such as Jackson Pollack, Willem de Kooning, Diego Rivera, and Ben Shahn, would later become leaders of the modern art movement.

Artist Ben Shahn painted in a style called social realism, which dealt with the problems of the poor. He also worked as a photographer for the government. *(Private Collection)*

The Federal Theater Project (FTP) became the most controversial of the Federal One projects because its director Hallie Flanagan wanted to deal with social issues, such as racial injustice, as well as entertain. One of FTP's most noted productions was Orson Welles's *Macbeth,* which was set in Haiti and starred an all-black cast. Many employees of the FTP also went on to become leaders in theater and film. They included Welles, playwright Arthur Miller, and directors John Houseman and John Huston. The FTP produced hundreds of plays and employed thousands of actors, writers, and stagehands. FTP crews toured the country providing free shows and even circuses. From 1935 to 1939, around 30 million Americans saw free FTP productions.

The Federal Writers' Project (FWP) produced more than 1,000 titles over four years, most of which were distributed to the public for free or at very low cost. Its most notable accomplishment was *Life in America,* a 150-volume set of American folklore and stories. Such famous American writers as Saul Bellow, John Cheever, Richard Wright, and Ralph Ellison got their start in the FWP.

About 15,000 musicians found work with the Federal Music Project (FMP). The project created hundreds of new orchestras and commissioned new works

Over his long career in theater and film, John Houseman was a producer, director, writer, and actor. *(Private Collection)*

Alan Lomax's research led to the Library of Congress Archive of Folk Song. Here he performs at a concert in Asheville, North Carolina. *(Library of Congress)*

Many states reacted to the poverty of the early depression with their own old-age pension programs. The national Social Security law was passed in 1935. *(Franklin D. Roosevelt Presidential Library and Museum)*

from composers. Some employees became teachers offering free music lessons to children, and one researcher, Alan Lomax, recorded hundreds of blues and folk songs from the rural South that might otherwise have been lost to history.

SOCIAL SECURITY

With the Social Security Act of 1935, Roosevelt answered critics and reformers such as Upton Sinclair and Dr. Francis Townsend who had proposed old-age pensions for America's elderly. The law went much further than Sinclair or Townsend's proposals, and Roosevelt considered it the greatest achievement of all his New Deal programs. First, Social Security provided a pension for Americans over age 65, which would be financed by both employees and employers. A percentage of a worker's salary was withheld and put into a fund for their future retirement. The employer matched this amount.

In the past, the elderly had relied on their savings, their family, or charity programs, but Roosevelt considered it the federal government's duty "to promote the general welfare," a phrase from the Constitution. For the bill to be passed, the president was forced to make a concession to southern members of Congress by excluding farm and domestic workers from the benefits. In this way, southern leaders excluded many African Americans from the program. Even so, Roosevelt managed to include other benefits in this landmark bill.

Social Security also created unemployment insurance for workers to give them an income if they lost their jobs. Both employee and employer again contributed to a fund for future use. Another benefit of the act was relief payments to the disabled to supplement inadequate state disability programs. It also provided for some financial aid for the children of poor families. The WPA and Social Security acts were huge accomplishments, but Roosevelt had several more plans for his second New Deal.

ADVENTURES IN THE COMIC STRIPS

Readers of all ages needed to escape the everyday fears of the depression as well, and the easiest way was to read the adventures of their comic strip heroes. During the 1930s, numerous new comic strips were appearing, and the most popular were the strips that told stories in daily or weekly installments. Heroes came in all forms: detective, athlete, space traveler, and apeman. Loyal readers followed their exploits all over the world or the universe. In the hard times of the depression, the usual message of the strips was that the good guy always wins.

The most popular detective was Dick Tracy, whose specialty was tommy-gunning gangsters. The strip was filled with gunfire every week. Kids loved saving cereal box tops, which they mailed in for official *Dick Tracy* badges. It was *Buck Rogers's* job to save the universe from archvillains, such as Killer Kane and Ardala in the year 2430. His wide array of cosmic weapons included rocket pistols and disintegrator guns. *Terry and the Pirates* featured the young hero Terry and his adult protector Pat Ryan as they battled the evil Dragon Lady in exotic far east Asian settings. The jungle adventures of *Tarzan, King of the Jungle* also captivated many kids who used the make-believe of the comics to escape the hard, real world.

The comic strips became so popular that the heroes appeared in radio shows, movies, and full-length comic books. An endless array of toys and clothes also appeared. When Macy's department store in New York City advertised the first Buck Rogers disintegrator gun for sale, 20,000 parents and kids showed up the next day to wait in line for the store to open.

Books sponsored by the FWP included travel guides, local histories, and nature studies. The poster above advertises an FWP history of Illinois. *(Library of Congress)*

LABOR, FARMERS, AND PUBLIC UTILITIES

In 1935 the Supreme Court declared the NRA unconstitutional because it gave legislative power to the president, rather than Congress. NRA price controls had meant fair wages and a limited workweek. Without the restrictions of the NRA, businesses resumed price wars. Lower prices meant lower wages and longer hours for workers. The American Federation of Labor estimated that more than 1 million workers were immediately affected by the end of the NRA by either lower wages or longer hours.

Roosevelt, however, gave labor an important victory in 1935 with the National Labor Relations Act. The bill was usually called the Wagner Act because New

"I would like to have it said of my first administration that in it the forces of selfishness and of lust for power met their match."

—FDR in the final speech of his 1936 presidential campaign

"A great forward step in that liberation of humanity which began with the Renaissance."

—Secretary of Labor Frances Perkins on the importance of the Social Security Act

Senator Robert Wagner of New York was a strong supporter of labor. As a result of his Wagner Act, organized labor rose from 3.5 million in 1935 to 15 million by 1947.
(Library of Congress)

York senator Robert. Wagner had first submitted the bill earlier in the year. The act gave workers the federal government's full support in organizing their own unions. It also required employers to recognize workers' unions. The bill set up the National Labor Relations Board to prevent unfair labor practices by employers and to negotiate contracts between labor and management when disputes occurred.

Roosevelt also addressed the gap left by the Supreme Court's dismantling of his AAA farmers' program. The Soil Conservation Act of 1935 restored payments to farmers, this time for soil conservation measures. The farmers were paid $1 an acre for planting fields of grasses rather than crops to restore nutrients to the soil and to prevent the topsoil erosion that had created the dust bowl. The Shelterbelt Project planted thousands of trees on the Great Plains to serve as windbreaks and help prevent another dust bowl.

Roosevelt was opposed to the power that the huge public utility holding companies had gained over the years without interference from state governments. He felt their control, similar to the power of a trust or a monopoly, was especially dangerous in a business where the public interest was so much at stake. The Public Utility Holding Company Act (also the Wheeler-Rayburn Act) gave the Securities and Exchange Commission the power to reduce the size of the companies and dissolve those that were not acting in the public interest. The SEC could also supervise the financial transactions of the companies.

Roosevelt put together his Revenue Act of 1935 as a response to Huey Long's Share Our Wealth program. His original bill called for huge increases in inheritance taxes and income taxes for both corporations and the wealthy. Long supported the original bill, but few others did. By the time the bill got through Congress, it only increased the top personal income tax from 59 percent to 75 percent and increased the estate and gift taxes of the wealthy.

THE BIGGEST MOVIE STAR OF THE 1930s

She made her movie debut in 1931 at the age of three and made $50. By 1935, she was the top box-office star in Hollywood, making more than $300,000 a year. More important, she probably did more to raise the hopes of Americans during the depression than anyone except perhaps President Roosevelt. She was Shirley Temple, the biggest child star Hollywood has ever seen.

Temple was first noticed with a song-and-dance routine in *Stand Up and Cheer* in 1934. She had the singing, dancing, and acting abilities of someone much older and a beaming, dimpled smile that made everyone forget their troubles. She also had curly blonde hair, which her mother made up with exactly 52 curls before each movie. Once America saw her, they could not get enough of her. She was the top box-office draw every year from 1935 through 1938,

Shirley Temple won an Academy Award in 1934 for her "outstanding contribution to film." Here, she celebrates a birthday with another Hollywood star, Eddie Cantor. *(Library of Congress)*

starring in 14 films and making $5 million a year for her studio. She starred in children's classics, such as *Heidi* and *Rebecca of Sunnybrook Farm,* in which eternal hope was always the theme, and there was always a happy ending.

Parents went Shirley-crazy, giving their daughters Shirley Temple hairdos and buying Shirley Temple clothes, books, and dolls. Despite the depression, more than 6 million Shirley Temple dolls were purchased during the 1930s. Shirley Temple once said, "I stopped believing in Santa Claus when my mother took me to see him at a department store and he asked me for my autograph." By 1940, Temple had grown up and her career started to fade. However, her films are still popular today, and she is also remembered by the children's drink named after her—a Shirley Temple is made of ginger ale, grenadine, and a cherry.

Finally, the Banking Act of 1935 gave the Federal Reserve Board the authority to regulate interest rates and control the economy. For example, when the economy slowed down, lower interest rates increase borrowing and stimulated the economy. When buying increased too much, higher interest rates decreased spending and prevented inflation. This bill made it clear that control of the economy had switched from the hands of business to the hands of the federal government.

This second New Deal is sometimes referred to as the second hundred days because all the legislation took place in one session of Congress from April to August 1935. The second New Deal was an impressive list of bills, but Americans had to wait to see how effective the laws would be in easing the lingering effects of the

"This generation of Americans has a rendezvous with destiny."

—President Roosevelt accepting his presidential renomination at the 1936 Democratic Convention

Some WPA projects were strange. One writer was given the job of taking a dog census in Monterey, California. That writer was John Steinbeck, who later wrote *The Grapes of Wrath,* the classic novel about the depression and emigrants from the dust bowl.

depression. In 1936, legislation slowed considerably as a presidential election and war news in Europe dominated the headlines.

ISOLATIONISM AND NEUTRALITY

With the strong support of both the people and his Democratic Congress, Roosevelt had the power to try to solve the huge problems of the depression. This was not true in his foreign policy. As Europe again headed toward war, Roosevelt wanted to rebuild the military, at least enough for self-defense, but the people were in no mood for any talk of war.

Feelings of isolationism were very strong for several reasons. Memories of World War I were still negative. More than 300,000 Americans had died in a war that seemed, by the 1930s, to have resolved nothing. After the war, the economy suffered for several years and the farmers had

THE RISE OF THE TEENAGER

One of the developments of the 1930s that affected American society for the rest of the century was the appearance of a teenage culture. Before the 1930s, teens were thought of as young adults because many had quit school and had jobs. During the depression, steps were taken to encourage teens to stay out of the job market, thus keeping unemployment numbers down. Roosevelt's National Youth Administration (NYA) gave grants of money to teens in return for school-related work to keep them in school until graduation.

The result was that teens stayed in school, most through high school graduation, and spent much more leisure time with each other. They started looking to each other, rather than family, for good times and advice. After all, the depression seemed to show that adults had not done a very good job of managing things. Also, the automobile gave teens much more mobility, which let them expand their experiences far beyond the family. The new concept

of dating away from family influence began to spread widely.

Once business noticed the trend toward a teen culture, there was an outburst of teen products, including teen clothes, foods, and magazines. Advertisers for these products usually appealed to the teenagers' desire for an increased social life and acceptance by fellow teens. By the late 1930s, the movie industry was making many growing up movies about teens. The most popular of these was the Andy Hardy series, starring actor Mickey Rooney as the typical American teen exploring responsibility, independence, and, most of all, girls. The first Andy Hardy movie was *A Family Affair* made in 1937. It was so popular that four more Andy Hardy movies were released in 1938; 15 were released all together. The series featured the simpler aspects of being a teen. Andy Hardy may not have been the most typical teen, but he was certainly the most well known.

not recovered yet. Many Americans were also upset by a 1934 Senate investigation, which revealed illegal profiteering by American arms manufacturers and bankers during World War I. Most important of all: There was still the war on the depression to win at home.

In response to the war winds in Europe, Congress passed the Neutrality Act in 1935. The act placed an embargo, or a government order forbidding commerce, on the transport of American weapons to any nations involved in a war. The law also denied protection to Americans traveling on the ships of nations at war. Roosevelt understood the clear feelings of the American people and signed the bill, but his speeches continued to warn of the dangers of remaining unprepared for war in Europe.

In 1936, **Margaret Mitchell's** *Gone With the Wind* **was published. The romantic novel about the effect of the Civil War on the South broke all sales records within six months.**

DICTATORS MAKE THE FIRST MILITARY MOVES

In Nazi Germany, Hitler continued to rebuild the military, threaten neighboring countries, and oppress the Jews. In March 1935, Hitler renounced the Treaty of Versailles and announced the creation of an army of 500,000 men through mandatory military service. In September 1935, he instituted the Nuremberg Laws, which stripped Jews of their German citizenship and outlawed marriages between Jews and Aryans (white, non-Jewish, northern Europeans). In March 1936, Hitler made his first military move by occupying the Rhineland, an area of Germany bordering France that had been made into a permanent demilitarized zone by the Treaty of Versailles. In October 1936, Hitler formed the Rome-Berlin Axis, an alliance with dictator Benito Mussolini's Italy, after the Italian conquest of Ethiopia.

The most disturbing event in Europe at this time was the Spanish Civil War of 1936–37. Democratic elections in Spain early in 1936 gave control of the government to a coalition of socialists and communists. At

An estimated 500,000 people died during the Spanish Civil War (1936–39). Above, Loyalist soldiers prepare to defend Madrid against Franco's Nationalists. *(AP/Wide World)*

"He's quite mad, but he might do good business cheaply."

—Italian leader Benito Mussolini after his first meeting with Adolf Hitler

the same time, there were strong anticommunist feelings in the country, especially in the military. For several months, there were street battles between opposing groups, peasant revolts, and strikes. In July, the military, led by anticommunist General Francisco Franco, tried to restore order by taking over the government. Troops loyal to the government resisted, and the Spanish Civil War began. Franco's anticommunist forces were called the Nationalists while the troops defending the socialist government were called Loyalists.

By the end of the year, both Germany and Italy recognized the Nationalist government, which Franco had set up in northern Spain. Roosevelt knew the Axis nations would soon be sending military support to Franco to overthrow the socialist Spanish government. Although it was doubtful that the Neutrality Act forbade U.S. involvement in a civil war, many isolationists in Congress strongly opposed any intervention. Roosevelt also had no support from France and England, who supported the Loyalists, and he also hesitated to take any action. It was a hesitation that would prove disastrous to the Loyalists. Axis troops were soon in Spain supporting the Nationalists. It was an omen of the bigger battle to come in Europe.

In late November 1936, Japan signed a pact with Germany and became the third member nation of the Axis. Both Germany and Japan agreed to consult on issues concerning the Soviet Union and to support each other in case of a Soviet attack. Japan's military had used the depression as an excuse to take control of the Japanese government in 1930 and began their own program of conquest and expansion. In 1931–32, Japan took control of Manchuria, China, as the first part of a plan to conquer all of China. The League of Nations condemned the invasion but had no power to prevent it. In 1933, Japan withdrew from the league.

"It is us today. It will be you tomorrow."

—Ethiopian emperor Haile Selassie to the League of Nations asking for support after Italy's invasion of his country

THE 1936 OLYMPICS

Americans experienced a special victory at the 1936 Olympic games held in Berlin, Germany. Hitler planned to use the Olympics as propaganda to support his racist Nazi views. He and his followers believed that Germans were part of a master race of Aryans. Hitler's fanatic beliefs led to demanding training programs for Germany's Olympic athletes. He desired to win nearly every gold medal at the games. Germany did win the most gold medals at the 1936 Olympics, but there was one American athlete who shattered Hitler's twisted dream.

Jesse Owens was a great U.S. track-and-field star who had set many world records during his career at

Hitler called his new Germany the Third Reich, or third empire, and claimed it would last more than 1,000 years.

Jesse Owens won four gold medals in the 1936 Olympics. In each event, Owens either tied or set new Olympic records. *(Library of Congress)*

The land speed record was broken on September 3, 1935, on the Bonneville Salt Flats in Utah. England's Malcolm Campbell hit 300 mph with his *Bluebird Special* racecar.

Ohio State University. He was also African American and, according to Hitler, racially inferior. When it came time for Owens's competition with the German track stars, Hitler was in attendance at the stadium to witness their victories. The first event was the 100-yard dash, and Owens defeated the German runner, setting a new world record. The huge German crowd was stunned into silence, and Hitler left the stadium before the awards ceremony for Owens. Owens went on to win three more gold medals at the games, and African-American athletes took home a total of 13 medals.

MINORITIES AND THE NEW DEAL

Despite these victories, African-American athletes came home to an America still bitterly divided over race. Eleanor Roosevelt was a staunch supporter of civil rights for African Americans, but President Roosevelt never made any effort to remove the segregation laws of the South as he had promised in his campaign. There is little doubt he believed in civil rights, but he also knew he would lose the support of the South if he acted on the issue, and as a result, be defeated for the presidency. The only stand Roosevelt would take on a civil rights issue was his support of an antilynching bill that was first introduced in Congress in 1934. The bill consistently died in the Senate after a filibuster by Southern senators. (A filibuster is a legislative strategy that delays or prevents a vote from occurring in the Senate. During a filibuster, senators take turns speaking for hours and hours on the floor of the Senate, sometimes about nothing pertaining to the bill. The group keeps speaking until the session closes without a vote on the bill.)

Roosevelt's New Deal programs helped many African Americans during the depression. Federal civil service jobs were opened to all qualified workers regardless of race or sex and 200,000 young African Americans found employment in the CCC. More than 400,000 African Americans learned to read and write as a result of a WPA program, and many African-American artists found work through the WPA's Federal One projects. African-American sharecroppers also took advantage of the labor union movement of the decade to form the Sharecroppers Union. By 1936, the union had more than 10,000 members.

Even within the New Deal programs, racism was still present, however. Salaries required by the NRA codes were higher for whites than African Americans. Nearly one-third of the New Deal subsidized housing

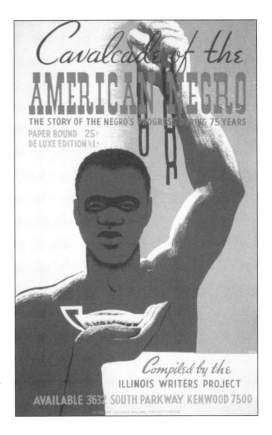

The depression hit African Americans especially hard, but the Illinois WPA sponsored this history of "the Negro's progress during 75 years."
(Library of Congress)

African-American sharecroppers received 70 percent less in relief payments than did white farmers.

In 1935, American aviator Amelia Earhart became the first person to fly across the Pacific from Hawaii to California.

In October 1936, the Boulder Dam was completed on the Nevada-Arizona border. Cooling tubes in the cement made the cement dry more quickly. Engineers estimate that using the old methods of drying cement would have required a century for the cement to harden.

units were built for African Americans, but almost all of the housing was segregated as were all the new WPA schools. African Americans received less than 10 percent of the homeowner loans and aid to education. Social Security excluded farmers and domestic workers, jobs commonly held by African Americans. In urban areas, the unemployment rates for African Americans remained around 30 percent, much higher than the rate for whites.

Nearly 500,000 women received jobs from the WPA, and the salary gap between men and women was narrowed by NRA codes. However, unemployment became a particular problem for married women during the depression because employers assumed that men were supporting the family. As a result, married women were often excluded from jobs to preserve positions for men.

One group that made significant social and economic improvement during the 1930s was Native Americans, due to the efforts of Roosevelt's Indian Commissioner John Collier. Collier brought special CCC camps to the reservations and built 84 day schools. He returned lands that had been taken away by the federal government. He also convinced Congress to pass the Indian Reorganization Act, which provided much more self-rule for American Indian tribes. Federal loans resulted in beneficial projects in irrigation, land restoration, and animal management. By the end of the 1930s, these improvements brought about a 55 percent decrease in the mortality rate on the reservations.

THE ECONOMY IMPROVES

By 1936, it looked like Roosevelt's New Deal programs were having an effect on the economy. Unemployment had been cut in half from 25 percent in 1933 to 13 percent. America's gross national product had increased from $485 per capita (per individual) in 1933 to $650 per capita in 1936, and production had doubled since 1932. Total income in the country was up from $40 billion in 1933 to $65 billion, and farmers' income was up by about 50 percent. Corporate profits had doubled since Roosevelt took office, and even the stock market, which had played such an important role in bringing on the depression, was up 80 percent. More than 3 million Americans were still on relief and 9 unemployed, but Roosevelt was ready to take his record for the last four years on the campaign trail to see if the people wanted to re-elect him for a second term.

THE 1936 ELECTION

Roosevelt's critics said he had not been able to break the depression's grip on the country. Unemployment and poverty were still high after four years of his New Deal. They criticized him for running the country into debt with programs that were only temporary fixes. Some accused him of turning the entire government into a socialist system. Some polls had him losing the presidency to the Republican nominee, Kansas governor Alfred Landon.

The 1934 elections were one indication that the American people thought Roosevelt was doing a good job. The 1936 election would prove to be an even greater show of support as Roosevelt was re-elected by the greatest margin in history up to that time. He carried every state but two, Maine and Vermont, winning the electoral college vote by 523 to 8. He won the popular vote by 27.5 million to 16.7 million.

The congressional elections increased the Democrats' majority in both the House and the Senate. Democrates now dominated the House by 333 to 88 and the Senate by 75 to 16. Roosevelt needed all the support he could get. There was still work to be done to end the depression and events in Europe were making all Americans fear another world war.

Governor Landon carried only two states in the 1936 presidential election. Landon actually supported many of President Roosevelt's New Deal programs. *(Library of Congress)*

After FDR's landslide victory in the 1936 election, Father Coughlin retired from politics. He later said his political career was the biggest mistake he ever made.

The jitterbug grew out of two earlier dances, the black bottom and Lindy Hop. Jitterbuggers performed acrobatic moves to popular swing music. *(Cornell Copa, Magnum Photos)*

"IT DON'T MEAN A THING IF IT AIN'T GOT THAT SWING"

The 1920s are often called the Jazz Age because of the general disregard for convention during that decade, not just because of jazz music. The phrase came to be associated with a general life style. Jazz music itself was very influential, but it was primarily African-American music and a deeply segregated America did not accept it completely. The music's popularity did not expand widely because many clubs were segregated, and most radio stations refused to play African-American music. The depression made it even tougher for African-American musicians, as their one source of exposure, recordings, also declined in sales due to the economy.

Times were tough for all musicians as the depression deepened, and many found the only way to make a living was to join one of the big bands of the early 1930s. The bands, both African American and white, traveled across the country playing wherever they could, usually in one-night-stands. As the big band trend developed, they were divided into two types. Sweet bands, such as those led by Guy Lombardo and Sammy Kaye, played easy music meant as a pleasant background to conversation or dinner. Swing bands, such as those of Benny Goodman and Count Basie, were more influenced by jazz and played more of an up-tempo style meant for dancing. Their music was a combination of pop music and jazz.

Swing music was a form of jazz. One popular swing band during the 1930s was the Count Basie Band performing below in Chicago's Savoy Ballroom. *(Library of Congress)*

Clarinetist Benny Goodman became known as "the King of Swing." Goodman grew up very poor in Chicago and was educated at Jane Addams's Hull-House. *(Library of Congress)*

"It is a fabulous country, the only fabulous country, it is the one place where miracles not only can happen but where they happen all the time."

—Novelist Thomas Wolfe on America in his novel *Of Time and the River*

In 1934, the Benny Goodman Band became part of a network radio show called *Let's Dance.* His part of the show was heard from 12:30 A.M. to 1:30 A.M. on the East Coast, but three hours earlier in prime time on the West Coast. In 1935, Goodman took his band on a coast-to-coast tour, but most audiences seemed to want to hear the old standards rather than swing. Los Angeles was the last stop on the tour, and Goodman's band started to play the old numbers, which they had been playing on the rest of the tour. Even that did not please the Los Angeles audience, and they told him why—they had heard his swing music on *Let's Dance* and had come just to hear that. The band played swing for the rest of the concert to a delighted audience, and swing music took off across the country from that night onward.

For the rest of the decade, America could not get enough swing. Radio and a new contraption found in bars and restaurants, the jukebox, spread the sound everywhere. Record sales soared as the economy improved, reaching more than $20 million in 1938. African-American band leader Duke Ellington said, "Jazz is music, swing is business." At swing concerts, young people danced in the aisles, doing a new fast and furious dance called the jitterbug.

Another important aspect of Goodman's band is that he was the first leader to integrate his band with great African-American musicians, such as Teddy Wilson on piano, Lionel Hampton on vibes, and Charlie Christian on guitar. When Goodman returned to New York, he gave a triumphant concert at the usually traditional Carnegie Hall, with white and African-American musicians playing side by side. The darker mood of World War II brought an end to the swing craze in the early 1940s, but in that short time, its mass appeal had an effect beyond the concert halls.

CHAPTER 6

END OF THE NEW DEAL AND APPEASEMENT, 1937–1938

PRESIDENT ROOSEVELT BEGAN HIS second term on a high note. He ended his first term signing a flurry of new bills, known as the second New Deal, to strengthen the fight against the hardships of the depression. He had also silenced many of his critics with the biggest landslide victory in the history of presidential elections.

In 1937, the WPA employed more than 3 million workers. Above is a school built by the WPA in Alamogordo, New Mexico. *(Library of Congress)*

Despite being a member of the KKK when he was young, Hugo Black became a strong supporter of Roosevelt's New Deal after his Supreme Court appointment in 1937. *(Library of Congress)*

"If we do not have the courage to lead the American people where they want to go, someone else will."

—President Roosevelt urging Congress to support his court-packing legislation

"We are under a Constitution but the Constitution is what the [Supreme Court] judges say it is."

—Chief Justice Charles Evans Hughes defending the Supreme Court during Roosevelt's court-packing controversy

Roosevelt had the overwhelming support of the American people, but he knew there was still much work to be done. He said in his inauguration speech, "I see one-third of a nation ill-housed, ill-clad, ill-nourished," and he promised to ask Congress to pass more New Deal laws to help those who were still suffering.

PACKING THE COURT

The only obstacle Roosevelt had left was the Supreme Court. The judges had overturned the NRA and the AAA, and they were indicating that there might also be constitutional problems with the Tennessee Valley Authority (TVA) and Social Security. Roosevelt did not want to spend time getting new programs approved only to have them overturned by the court. His attempted solution to the problem would turn out to be one of the biggest mistakes of his presidency.

Roosevelt proposed to Congress that changes be made to the judicial system. He hoped to add new judges throughout the federal courts. The legislation would eventually add 44 judges to the lower courts and 6 judges to the Supreme Court. Roosevelt said the increase in the number of judges would help a system overloaded with cases and add new blood, but his real intention was clear to everyone. If he were able to appoint his own judges to the Supreme Court, he was certain his New Deal programs would not be overturned.

Roosevelt probably anticipated opposition from the Court and from Republicans in Congress, but even most of his fellow Democrats were outraged at his apparent disregard for the balance of power in the federal government among the executive, legislative, and judicial branches. Democrats were also upset that he did not consult them before announcing his proposal. Polls showed that the president did not even have the support of the public on his court- packing plan; many people accused him of trying to overturn the constitutional system of government.

For the first half of 1937, the debate went on while little else got done. Roosevelt continued to push Congress on the legislation when it was clear he had little support for it there. A Senate committee called it "needless, futile, and utterly dangerous." In the meantime, only minor New Deal legislation was passed. The Farm Tenancy Act made it easier for small farmers to obtain federal loans. The Wagner Housing Act authorized federal loans for the building of low-rent housing units. The Revenue Act of 1937 eliminated forms of tax evasion used by the wealthy. This legislation was all far less than what Congress might have accomplished without the judicial reform debate.

The issue resolved itself in May 1937 when Justice Willis Van Devanter, one of the Supreme Court's main opponents to the New Deal, resigned. Roosevelt was able to appoint Senator Hugo Black, a New Deal supporter, to the Court. As the balance of power shifted, the one-vote swing was enough to eliminate the Court as an obstacle to Roosevelt's plans. However, much damage had been done. An entire session of Congress was wasted over the furor, and the New Deal lost most of its momentum. The public's trust in the president was also shaken for the first time.

A 1937 editorial cartoon pokes fun at Roosevelt's plan to pack the Supreme Court with six extra judges to support his New Deal policies. *(Library of Congress)*

LABOR'S NEW WEAPON: THE SIT-DOWN STRIKE

Despite the Wagner Act's requirement that employers recognize unions, big businesses still found ways around the law. The United Automobile Workers (UAW) union was formed in 1935, but General Motors (GM) was determined to avoid unionization and spent almost $1 million between 1934 and 1936 to break the union. GM was the country's largest industrial employer, with 250,000 workers at plants throughout the country. The UAW wanted union recognition and better working conditions from GM, but the company would not

"I shall oppose it, but I don't imagine it'll do any good. Why, if the president asked Congress to commit suicide tomorrow, they'd do it."

—Senator Carter Glass opposing FDR's court-packing legislation and the president's control over Congress

Swing dance started at the Savoy Ballroom in the Harlem section of New York City. The club opened in 1926 and remained the top of its class until it closed 32 years later. The heyday of jitterbugging came in the 1930s.

The first full-length animated movie, Walt Disney's *Snow White and the Seven Dwarfs*, opened in December 1937. The film's $1.5 million cost drove the Disney studio close to bankruptcy, but the film earned much more than that in its first year alone.

negotiate with the union. Starting in late 1936, UAW workers at several plants staged sit-down strikes.

A sit-down strike was a new tactic used by workers in which they stopped work while also occupying the plants and factories of their employers. There were two main reasons that this type of strike was more effective than other strikes. First, with union members inside the plant, employers could not hire other workers (called *scabs* by the union workers) to enter the plants and keep production going. Also, employers were less likely to hire strikebreakers or ask the police to use violence against the strikers inside because it might damage plant equipment.

The most important plant in the UAW strike was in Flint, Michigan, the company's town. When local courts refused to evict the strikers in January 1937, GM felt they had no choice but to use force. The police used tear gas, billy clubs, and guns to attack the plant. The workers forced the police back by using the plant's fire hoses and throwing heavy car parts. Two more police attacks failed, though the gunfire wounded several strikers. The next morning 10,000 nonunion workers showed up to join the union.

After four months of no production, GM management decided they could no longer afford the loss of profits. GM recognized the workers' union and negotiations resulted in a shorter workweek, higher pay, and a reasonable speed of production for the workers. It was a significant victory for labor.

One month later, U.S. Steel finally accepted the steelworkers' union and gave the steelworkers a 40-hour workweek and a wage increase. Soon, other big companies, including Firestone Tire and Rubber, General Electric, and RCA, recognized their workers' unions. By the end of 1937, the number of union members had increased by hundreds of thousands. Two more bloody labor battles remained, however.

Auto manufacturer Henry Ford continued to resist union organization in his Ford Motor Company shops

Henry Ford constantly violated the Wagner Act, which gave workers the right to unionize. Here, Ford agents beat up union organizers at a 1937 strike. *(Library of Congress)*

and placed hundreds of spies on the production lines. He also had a factory police force, which he called the "service department," and he installed microphones throughout his factories to eavesdrop on all conversations. To deal with diminishing sales and profits during the depression, Ford increased the speed of the production lines and banned all talking, whistling, and singing. In May 1937, these working conditions made the workers at the River Rouge, Michigan, plant call in UAW organizers to help them unionize. Ford agents beat up the organizers, and Ford managed to avoid unionization once again. It would not be until

By the end of 1937, nearly 8 million Americans belonged to unions that had contracts guaranteeing wages, hours, and safety measures.

Violence between workers and police became a common scene during the thousands of labor strikes that took place in the 1930s. *(Library of Congress)*

In 1937, pilot Amelia Earhart disappeared during a flight from New Guinea to Howland Island in the Pacific Ocean. She and navigator Fred Noonan were attempting to be the first to fly around the world. No trace of the plane was ever found.

a huge workers' strike in 1941 that Ford would finally recognize the UAW in his plants.

On Memorial Day 1937, that same month, one of the most deadly labor confrontations took place in Chicago, Illinois, at the Republic Steel plant. The striking steelworkers were picketing outside the plant when one worker threw a stick at the police. When the police fired gunshots into the air, the strikers reacted by throwing more rocks and sticks. The police opened fire on the workers and chased them as they tried to flee. Ten

A WILD NIGHT OF THEATER

The Federal Theater Project of the WPA seemed like a great idea for everyone involved. Actors, writers, and stagehands had jobs. Theater owners were very happy to be able to rent out their buildings again because most had been forced to close since the depression started. Audiences all over America got to see free plays, many of them produced by the best people in the business, such as producers Orson Welles and John Houseman and writer Marc Blitzstein. The staging of Blitzstein's musical *The Cradle Will Rock,* however, created a real life drama equal to the play.

On June 16, 1937, *The Cradle Will Rock* was scheduled to premiere at the Maxine Eliot Theater in New York City. The federal government had gotten many complaints about communists within the FTP and their staging of anticapitalist plays. In the 1930s, a prounion stand was sometimes enough to also be labeled procommunist, and *The Cradle Will Rock* definitely had a prounion theme. WPA officials sent government troops to lock up the Maxine Eliot Theater and prevent the performance.

The play's producers and performers would not be discouraged. The crew and the audience marched down the streets of New York City to the Venice Theater, which was glad to have the business. Union rules forbade the actors from taking the stage, so Blitzstein narrated from a piano on the stage while the cast performed from the audience with no sets or costumes. It was an unusual night at the theater that emphasized the play's theme: the people's struggle for power.

The first Superman comic appeared in June 1938. The writer and illustrator, Jerry Siegel and Joe Shuster, each made $15 a week for their creation.

---

strikers were killed and 30 were wounded by the gunfire. Another 28 workers were hospitalized after being beaten by the police. The press referred to the labor battle as the Memorial Day Massacre. The workers were forced to return to work two months later without their union.

THE ECONOMY WEAKENS

After his Supreme Court disaster, Roosevelt suffered another blow in 1937 as the economy faltered once again. For the first part of the year, the economy strengthened as production, stocks, and wages all increased. Some economists were hopeful that the depression was almost over. In the background of these gains, however, the

RADIO POWER

Detective stories and adventures were popular radio fare, but one science fiction program frightened its listeners even more than it intended. On Halloween, October 31, 1938, Orson Welles's Mercury Theater presented author H. G. Wells's *The War of the Worlds* as if a real invasion from Mars were taking place. Some listeners panicked, boarding up their homes or running into the streets screaming in fear of the imagined attack. The program revealed the kind of fears that many Americans lived through during the 1930s.

On May 27, 1937, the Golden Gate Bridge opened in California, connecting San Francisco to Marin County. At the time, it was the longest suspension bridge in the world.

A worker looks out from the north tower of the Golden Gate Bridge during construction.
(Library of Congress)

unemployment rate of 11 percent and the number of families on relief at 4.5 million stayed steady. Industrialists seemed distrustful of the recovery, and their investments in the expansion remained very low.

Roosevelt was encouraged by the economic signs as the year started and decided to balance the federal budget by cutting back on federal relief programs and public works. He had always intended for many of the programs to be temporary fixes until the economy improved. The cutbacks, however, revealed how weak the economy still was and showed how its performance depended on the federal programs. By August, the economy was in big trouble again.

The main cause of the plunge in the economy, often called the Roosevelt recession, was the sudden removal of billions of dollars from circulation. Roosevelt's cutbacks withdrew $4 billion, and the new Social Security program removed another $2 billion as money was taken out of workers' wages and held in reserve for the future. The withdrawal of money created a snowball effect similar to the beginning of the depression. Less money meant that consumer spending decreased. As spending decreased, production fell off. Between August and October, stocks fell 40 percent and between August and December, 2 million workers lost their jobs.

Roosevelt waited to see if the economy might stabilize on its own, but it did not. By April 1938, another 2 million people had lost their jobs, and Roosevelt's economic advisers told him that two-thirds of the recovery achieved since 1933 had been lost. He immediately asked Congress to approve $2 billion for the WPA and other programs, $1 billion for government loans, and $2 billion in cash from the gold reserves. Congress approved and added another $1.5 billion for the Reconstruction Finance Corporation (RFC) bringing the total to $6.5 billion to be invested back into the economy. Results were almost immediate; by the end of the year, production was up, unemployment was down,

CAFÉ SOCIETY

Not everyone suffered during the depression. Many fortunes had been wiped out by the 1929 stock market crash, but America still had its rich upper class. Some of the old families, such as the Astors and Vanderbilts, were still prospering, but some new elements of society had joined them. America's bad times meant good times for many movie stars as Americans still flocked to the theaters to enjoy the escapism of the movies and to see their favorite stars. Many of Europe's royalty, deposed after World War I, managed to escape to the United States with their wealth and their now meaningless titles to join America's new upper class, usually called café society.

Socialite Elsa Maxwell was called "the hostess with the mostest" for her flamboyant parties. *(Library of Congress)*

royalty. She was a songwriter and professional hostess from Keokuk, Iowa, who experience throwing parties for royalty and those in high society.

Another important group in café society was the debutantes, the young ideal beauties of the decade, often referred to as glamour girls. These young unmarried women were introduced to society at special events called coming-out parties or debuts, which often cost as much as $60,000—an enormous sum in the 1930s. The parties received a huge amount of publicity, and because many young girls dreamed of one day being as glamorous as the debutantes, they loved to hear and read about them. Nightclub owners invit-

The cafés where the new rich flaunted their wealth included New York City clubs such as the Stork Club, El Morocco, and 21. Many of the clubs were former speakeasies, and some were still run by gangsters, who would sometimes socialize with their café society customers. The social director for many café society parties was Elsa Maxwell. Maxwell was not from any of the old rich families or a movie star or European

ed the debutantes to their clubs for the publicity, so the young women would be out on the town most nights. Their adoring fans followed them closely in the newspapers, paying special attention to their new gowns and escorts. The publicity, parties, and debuts let these rich, young women exhibit themselves as charming, beautiful, and popular. Eventually most of them married wealthy young bachelors from their social circle.

and the recovery was back on track. Roosevelt, however, did not have his balanced budget.

Congress passed three other notable bills at Roosevelt's urging during its 1938 session. First, a new AAA bill was passed with only minor, re-establishing the agency struck down by the Supreme Court. The Fair Labor Standards Act created an immediate minimum wage of 25 cents an hour, which would increase to 40 cents an hour in seven years. The act also mandated a 40-hour workweek and time-and-a-half wages for overtime and reinstituted the ban on child labor. (This

THE *HINDENBURG* GOES UP IN FLAMES

In the mid-1930s, travelers were enjoying a new form of passenger air transportation called the dirigible, or zeppelin. The dirigible consisted of a huge bag of lighter-than-air gas, such as hydrogen or helium, and a gondola, or compartment, below for carrying crew and passengers, as well as an engine for propulsion. The most famous dirigible at the time was the huge German airship the *Hindenburg.*

The airship *Hindenburg* explodes over Lakehurst, New Jersey, in 1937. Sixty-one passengers' miraculously survived. *(Private Collection)*

As the *Hindenburg* approached Lakehurst, New Jersey, for its landing on May 6, 1937, everything seemed to be going well. It was just 200 feet above the ground, and a ground crew was guiding it to its landing area. Suddenly, the rear of the ship burst into flames and spread quickly forward as the hydrogen ignited. As it fell to earth, the ground crew ran and passengers and crew jumped from the gondola to escape the

The *Hindenburg* was more than 800 feet long and held seven million cubic feet of hydrogen gas. It could carry 100 passengers and crew, and by 1937, it had made 36 trips across the Atlantic Ocean. The airship flew at 80 miles per hour, and the trip across the Atlantic took around 60 hours to complete. Passengers paid $400 for a one-way trip and $720 for a round-trip flight. Flying on the *Hindenburg* was very comfortable, but one rule was strictly enforced—there was no smoking because the hydrogen gas was extremely explosive.

flames. It took only five minutes for the fire to burn itself out and completely destroy the *Hindenburg,* killing 36 people.

The cause of the fire was never determined, but one theory was sabotage. Germany's Nazi leader Adolf Hitler was proud of the *Hindenburg* as a symbol of Germany's growing strength and technology. However, one spark was all it took to embarrass Hitler and bring the brief age of the passenger airship to an end.

On March 18, 1938, a New London, Texas, school exploded and burned to the ground. The tragedy killed 500 people, mostly children.

time the ban on child labor was not overturned by the Supreme Court.) This act was the last major New Deal bill passed by Congress and signed by Roosevelt. Finally, Roosevelt also persuaded Congress to pass a bill increasing military spending, which approved $1.2 billion to expand the navy. The war drums in Europe were louder than ever.

APPEASEMENT IN EUROPE

As 1937 started, the civil war in Spain between the Loyalists and the Nationalists was at a stalemate. Neither side was winning. Roosevelt supported the Loyalists, who were defending an elected government, but he was prevented from supplying aid by the Neutrality Act. Hitler and Mussolini supported Franco and the Nationalists (who were also called Fascists) and provided military aid. By April, there were 100,000 Italian troops fighting with their fellow fascists. Hitler sent the 6,000 men of the German Condor Legion air force.

In late April, the legion bombed the civilian city of Guernica, Spain, killing more than 1,600 people. After this incident, support for the Loyalists grew in the United States. Eleanor Roosevelt spoke out strongly in favor of the Loyalists. American writers and Loyalist supporters Ernest Hemingway and John Dos Passos went to Spain to report on the war. Hundreds of men made their way from the United States to Spain to join the Loyalists on the battlefields.

By 1938, there were 3,000 Americans fighting in Spain, and they became known as the Abraham Lincoln Brigade. Still, isolationism remained strong among most Americans. In Washington, D.C., when Congress extended the Neutrality Act to include civil wars, Roosevelt signed the bill. When both England and France choose to remain neutral also, the fate of the Loyalists was sealed. By the end of 1938, the Nationalists and Franco were on the verge of victory and a government takeover.

In 1938, Hitler also revealed his intention to defend the rights of German people living in the bordering countries of Austria and Czechoslovakia. Hitler said that he was defending the rights of Germans in foreign lands, but other leaders in Europe knew that this was a threat to invade those two countries and unify them with Germany. The problem area in Czechoslovakia was the Sudetenland, a province on the Czech-German border that was inhabited mostly by Germans who supported Hitler. In Austria, the issue was the large number of German-Austrians in the country, due to the long history

> **M**ore than 40,000 men and women from 54 different countries volunteered to fight with the Loyalists in the Spanish Civil War. Because of their inexperience, many were wounded in their first days in battle.

Neville Chamberlain returns home with the disastrous Munich Agreement. Hitler also considered the pact a mistake because it delayed the start of the war. *(Library of Congress)*

of interaction between two bordering nations. The German-Austrians desired reunification with Germany, a union forbidden by the Treaty of Versailles, and they strongly supported Hitler.

Hitler eventually demanded of the Austrian leader, Chancellor Kurt von Schuschnigg, that more power be given to German-Austrian Nazis in the Austrian government. Schuschnigg agreed, but then tried to settle the issue once and for all by calling for a plebiscite—a vote of all the people—asking the Austrians whether they wanted to remain independent or join Germany. Hitler did not wait for the results of the vote. German troops invaded Austria on March 12, meeting little resistance. The next day, Hitler announced that Austria had been annexed, or had become part of Germany.

Britain and France accepted the annexation, knowing that war would have been the only way to stop it. This acceptance or appeasement of Hitler's actions avoided immediate war, but it also made Hitler believe he could get away with his demands without real opposition. He turned his sights next on Czechoslovakia and the Sudetenland. First, he massed his troops on the Czech border in a clear preparation for invasion. The military buildup resulted in a series of negotiations, mostly between Hitler and British prime minister Neville Chamberlain, in which Hitler demanded that the Sudetenland be ceded, or granted, to Germany. The situation was particularly alarming because both Britain and France had promised to defend Czechoslovakia's border militarily.

In a final meeting between Hitler and Chamberlain in Munich, Germany, on September 29–30, Chamberlain agreed to the ceding of the Sudetenland in return for Hitler's promise that there would be no more territorial demands. The appeasement came to be known as the Munich Agreement, through which Hitler gained control of more land and people without opposition. Chamberlain returned home to Britain saying the agree-

Nazi officials raise their flag after Germany's takeover of Austria in 1938. Austria had strong historical ties to Germany and was Adolf Hitler's birthplace. *(Library of Congress)*

ment meant "peace in our time." Many others knew it was a disaster. Hitler was not through with his demands.

JAPAN ATTACKS CHINA

In July 1937, Japan used a small clash between Japanese forces and Chinese civilians near the Manchurian border to justify a full invasion of China. In August, Japan occupied Beijing (then called Peking) and later set up a puppet government controlled by Japan. In November, Shanghai fell to Japanese troops after the Chinese army lost 270,000 troops defending the city. In December, Japanese troops occupied Nanking and

Japanese soldiers march into Nanking, China, after that city fell in 1937. Roosevelt wanted to supply China with arms but the Neutrality Act forbid it. *(AP/Wide World)*

sank an American gunboat in a convoy of oil tankers, killing 3 Americans and injuring 43. A major conflict with the United States was avoided when the Japanese government apologized to America and agreed to pay damages. However, the occupation of Nanking came to be called the Rape of Nanking after an estimated 200,000 Chinese civilians were murdered by Japanese troops.

Throughout 1938, Japanese troops pushed deeper into China from the north and east easily defeating the untrained Chinese troops. In an act of desperation in June, Chinese forces opened up the dikes of the Yellow River allowing the river to flood. The flood stalled the advance of Japanese troops, but it also killed many Chinese civilians who lived in the area. By the end of the year, the Chinese leader Generalissimo Chiang Kai-shek had withdrawn his troops into the mountains, and Japan occupied most of eastern China.

HITLER'S WAR AGAINST THE JEWS

The persecution of Jews in Nazi Germany also reached a crisis stage in 1938. After the annexation of Austria, the Nazis started sending most Jews to concentration camps. At this time, the camps were really prisons where the prisoners performed forced labor, often dying from mistreatment. In October, Nazis confiscated the property of 10,000 Polish Jews and deported them. Ten days after the deportation, the son of one of the Polish families shot and killed a German diplomat in Paris.

On November 10 throughout Germany, the Nazis organized what they called demonstrations against the Jews for the assassination. The demonstrations

> *"We are determined to keep out of war, but ... it is impossible for any nation to completely isolate itself."*
>
> —President Roosevelt's reaction to Japan's invasion of China

The morning after Kristallnacht, a woman walks by the broken windows of Jewish stores. *(AP/Wide World)*

turned violent as planned, and thousands of Jewish homes, synagogues, and shops were attacked and destroyed. Ninety Jews were killed and many others injured on the night that came to be known as *Kristallnacht,* or Night of the Broken Glass.

The next day, the Nazi government said that the Jews were responsible for the destruction on Kristallnacht and arrested 20,000 to be sent to concentration camps. All of Germany's remaining 500,000 Jews were fined 1 billion marks to pay for the damage, payable to the German government. There was no response from Britain or France. In Washington, Roosevelt granted permits to 15,000 German and Austrian refugees, mostly Jews, allowing them to stay in the United States.

JOSEPH STALIN

The 1930s saw the rise of another dictator who was, in some ways, even more brutal than Germany's Adolf Hitler. He was Joseph Stalin. The rest of the world did not become aware of his brutality until many years later because of the extreme secrecy of the Soviet government. Before his rule was over, he would be responsible for the deaths of millions of his own people.

Stalin became the dictator of the Soviet Union in 1929, five years after the death of Vladimir Lenin, the leader of the 1917 communist revolution. (Prior to the revolution, the nation was known as Russia, which is actually the name of one of its largest regions. Even after it officially became the Union of Soviet Socialist Republics [USSR], or the Soviet Union, many continued to refer to the entire nation as Russia.) One of Stalin's first acts was to collectivize, or join together, all farms under the control of the government. Farmers revolted against the takeover and destroyed half of the country's livestock and produce. As punishment, Stalin sent millions of the farmers and their families into exile in a harsh area of the Soviet Union called Siberia. Most of the exiles died there. The destruction of food also caused a widespread famine that claimed millions of lives.

In 1935, Stalin started a purge, or elimination, of anyone who threatened his rule. This group even included Communist allies and Soviet citizens who voiced opposition to Stalin. Millions of Soviet citizens (estimates range anywhere between 2 million and 7 million), including many in his military command, were arrested and executed between 1935 and 1938. Millions more were exiled. The purge left Stalin with only loyal officials around him, but the military was severely weakened, which would play a vital role during the early stages of the coming war.

Joseph Stalin (right) plays cards with Hitler's foreign minister Joachim von Ribbentrop in 1939. The two sides had just agreed to share dominance of eastern Europe. *(Library of Congress)*

THE JITTERBUG

Jitterbugging is as American as apple pie. Like many American musical styles and traditions, this dance craze developed and flourished in primarily African-American venues, then spread throughout the country, and eventually, the world.

This particular dance evolved directly from the Lindy Hop of the 1920s, in which the male dancer often took a solo turn, showing off acrobatic jumps. This airborne aspect may have contributed to the name Lindy, taken from famous aviator Charles Lindbergh. The physical demands required great agility and skill.

By 1936, the Lindy Hop was out, and jitterbugging was in. Danced to swing music made popular by Benny Goodman and similar bands, jitterbugging was vigorous, fresh, and simpler than the Lindy Hop. At places like the Savoy, which featured a block-long dance floor and a raised stage, hundreds of jitter-buggers a night filled the club.

Two jitterbuggers show off their style at the Savoy Ballroom in Harlem, ca. 1938. *(Library of Congress)*

THE FIGHT OF THE DECADE

One of the most important fights in the history of boxing took place on June 22, 1938, when Joe Louis met Max Schmeling for the heavyweight championship of the world. The fight became a symbol of the world battle between the supposed Aryan superiority of Hitler's Germany and the tolerance of democracies, such as that found in the United States. Louis was the heavyweight champion of the world and an African American. Schmeling was one of Hitler's most prized athletes, a fighter Hitler pointed to as proof of Aryan superiority. Schmeling was the former heavyweight champion and

Du Pont researcher Wallace Carothers invented nylon, the first manufactured fiber. One of its first uses was for women's stockings because it was much cheaper to use than silk.

Joe Louis knocks out Max Schmeling in the first round of their rematch in 1938. Louis was heavyweight champion 1937–49, longer than any other boxer. *(AP/Wide World)*

In 1938, a pilot named Douglas Corrigan took off from New York to fly nonstop to California. In a heavy fog, Corrigan lost his way and wound up flying instead across the Atlantic to Dublin, Ireland. He returned to America a hero and would forever be called "Wrong-Way" Corrigan.

had handed Louis his only defeat two years before with a twelfth-round knockout, before Louis won the championship. After the fight, Schmeling returned to Germany a hero.

As the rematch drew near, Louis knew there was more than just a heavyweight title at stake. A few weeks before the fight, President Roosevelt told Louis, "Joe, we're depending on those muscles for America." Louis did not disappoint. As 22 million Americans listened on their radios, Louis knocked Schmeling out in the first round, retaining his title and sending a strong message to Nazi Germany about Aryan superiority. Two years earlier, another African-American athlete, Jesse Owens, had delivered the same message with his victories at the 1936 Olympics in Berlin.

Pilot "Wrong Way" Corrigan studies a map after turning the wrong way on a flight to California. *(Library of Congress)*

CHAPTER 7

THE WAR BEGINS AND AMERICA STRUGGLES WITH NEUTRALITY, 1939

FOREIGN POLICY DOMINATED ROOSEVELT'S presidency in 1939 for the first time since he took office. By the end of 1938, he was certain the United States would not be able to avoid being part of the war that was clearly coming. Roosevelt strongly opposed the Neutrality Act, but isolationists still controlled Congress and spoke for the majority of Americans. In December 1938, Roosevelt approved the secret sale of 1,000 warplanes to France. Two weeks later, during his

The Elmore Thomas family prepares to leave Oklahoma for California in July 1939. Despite omens of war overseas, the depression was still a major fact of life for many Americans.
(Library of Congress)

After Hitler and Mussolini sent military support to Franco's Nationalists, the tide turned. Here, a lone Loyalist carries on the fight in Tervel, Spain. *(Library of Congress)*

> *"This nation will remain a neutral nation, but I cannot ask that every American remain neutral in thought as well. Even a neutral cannot be asked to close his mind or close his conscience."*
>
> —FDR on U.S. neutrality as war loomed in Europe

State of the Union address, he again warned of the dangers of isolationism. He also asked for more money for national defense and a revision of the Neutrality Act. Several more developments in Europe would have to take place before Congress finally agreed.

SPAIN AND CZECHOSLOVAKIA FALL

In March 1939, Franco's Nationalist forces captured Madrid and took control of the government, ending the Spanish Civil War. Britain and France both recognized the new fascist government. Roosevelt recalled the U.S. ambassador to Spain and urged Franco to avoid reprisals. However, Franco immediately ordered the execution of hundreds of Loyalists.

Also in March, Hitler completed the occupation of Czechoslovakia by sending German and Hungarian

THE TRAGEDY OF THE SS ST. LOUIS

On May 23, 1939, 934 Jewish refugees embarked from Hamburg, Germany, aboard the SS St. Louis trying to escape the horror of Nazi persecution. Each passenger had a visa for Cuba, where the refugees thought they would have a short stay before being allowed to enter the United States. Before they arrived, Cuba changed its immigration laws, and the refugees, mostly families with children, were not allowed to leave the ship.

The ship sailed the seas off the coast of Florida for several days awaiting word that the U.S. government would offer them refuge. President Roosevelt received many telegrams from sympathetic Americans asking him to allow the ship to land. The immigration laws at the time forbade the refugees' entry into the country. The ship sailed to Canada, but was once again turned away. The ship sought a home for the refugees for three weeks without success.

The captain finally had no choice but to sail back to Europe. The ship was granted temporary entry into Belgium. Nazi Germany soon conquered Belgium and controlled almost all of Europe, and they had only one plan for all Jews—extermination in concentration camps. Before the end of World War II, half the passengers on the SS St. Louis, including the children, would be dead.

Italy's leader Benito Mussolini founded the first Fascist movement in 1919. He would be overthrown and murdered in 1945 after military defeat in World War II. *(Library of Congress)*

troops into the remaining provinces. In April, Italy conquered Albania, putting Italian troops in a position to invade Greece. Britain and France again accepted the occupations, but British prime minister Chamberlain finally realized Hitler's intentions and swore to defend militarily the independence of Poland, Greece, and Romania.

Throughout early 1939, Japan continued its conquest of China. By March, Japan controlled Hainan, an island province in the southeast of China where naval invasions of such neighboring countries as the Philippines could easily be launched. Finally, in August, the Allies suffered a surprising blow. The Soviet Union and its leader Joseph Stalin, who was thought to be a potential ally against the Axis countries, signed a nonaggression pact with Hitler's Germany. The two countries promised no military action against each

"If Hitler wins in Europe—if the strength of the British and French armies and navies is forever broken—the United States will find itself alone in a barbaric world."

—U.S. playwright Robert Sherwood urging military aid to the Allies

"Democracy has disappeared in several other great nations, not because the people of those nations disliked democracy, but because they had grown tired of unemployment and insecurity, of seeing their children hungry while they sat helpless in the face of government confusion and government weakness."

—FDR on the rise of dictators around the world

other for 10 years. The real purpose of the pact was even more threatening and kept secret at the time. The two leaders both agreed to both invade Poland and split the country between them. Germany also would claim Lithuania while the Soviet Union was granted Finland, Latvia, and Estonia. In mid-1939, four Axis powers were carrying out plans for world conquest while the rest of the world just stood by and watched.

The isolationists in America stood firm throughout all these developments. There was debate in Congress about amending the Neutrality Act, but there was little support, and Congress adjourned in August. Roosevelt was able to terminate a 1911 treaty with Japan in which the United States supplied Japan with huge amounts of steel and other materials used in building ships and weapons. Otherwise, he could do little but issue official statements of protest. Roosevelt also sent personal messages to Hitler and Mussolini, including a list of 33 European and Middle Eastern countries that he wanted them to pledge not to invade. The two dictators ridiculed Roosevelt's request.

GERMANY INVADES POLAND

On September 1, 1939, just one week after Germany and the Soviet Union signed the nonaggression pact, German troops stormed into Poland. Two days later, Britain and France each declared war on Germany and World War II began. That same day, a German submarine sank the British ship *Athenia* off the coast of Scotland, killing 112, including 28 Americans. According to the Neutrality Act, the Americans were traveling beyond the protection of the U.S. government, so no action was taken in response.

On September 17, Soviet troops attacked Poland from the west. Britain and France decided not to send troops to Poland, but mobilized their militaries in France, anticipating a German invasion there. Alone,

the Polish army was no match for either invading force. Some of the Polish soldiers fought on horseback with lances instead of guns. On September 28, Warsaw (the Polish capital) surrendered, and Poland was divided between Germany and Russia as Hitler and Stalin had agreed one month earlier.

Despite a 1934 German-Polish nonaggression pact, Nazi troops invaded Poland on September 1, 1939. It was the start of World War II. *(Library of Congress)*

In late September, Roosevelt called Congress into session to revise the Neutrality Act. Despite the invasion of Poland, isolationism still remained strong in the United States. Roosevelt however, had new support to revise the act. First, it was clear that the U.S. embargo against selling arms to the countries at war was only hurting the Allies; Germany's military strength was far superior to Britain and France's. Also, the American people were changing their minds. They still did not want U.S. troops involved, but polls showed 84 percent wanted the Allies to win while just 2 percent favored the Axis. Sixty percent favored the repeal of the Neutrality Act.

THE MOST POWERFUL WEAPON OF ALL TIME

In January 1939, two German scientists published an article in a German scientific journal. They had found a way to create nuclear fission, the splitting of the atom. Scientists around the world instantly became alarmed. They knew that nuclear fission made vast amounts of energy and might be used to power weapons more powerful than the world had ever seen. Later that month, a conference of physicists was held in Washington, D.C., where the findings were confirmed. Nuclear fission had the potential to create incredibly destructive bombs, and Hitler's Germany had a head start on developing weapons based on fission.

The physicists immediately contacted the U.S. military about the potential of nuclear fission, but their news was met with little interest. U.S. military officials treated the news as if it were some kind of futuristic science fiction. The scientists decided they must inform President Roosevelt, but they needed someone of importance to deliver the message. In August, they convinced the most famous scientist in the world, physicist Albert Einstein, to contact the president.

Einstein wrote a letter to the president urging him to aid U.S. scientists in their experiments so that America could develop fission-based atomic weapons before Germany. Einstein was famous for his theory of relativity, and he was a Jewish refugee from Germany. He did not want to see weapons developed from nuclear fission, but he knew what would happen if the Nazis developed the bomb first.

The letter was finally delivered to President Roosevelt by one of his advisers, Leonard Sachs, in October. The president was unsure of its importance, but he appointed a committee to look into the issue. Three weeks later, the committee recommended that funding be granted for research on nuclear fission for military purposes. The president did not act until June 1940, after Germany's takeover of France, when he established the National Defense Research Committee to coordinate nuclear fission research projects. The research led to the United States becoming the first nation to develop the nuclear bomb, which it eventually used to end World War II.

Einstein fled Nazi Germany in 1933. He strongly urged President Roosevelt to develop atomic weapons, but he did not take part in their development. *(Library of Congress)*

On November 3, Congress passed a revised Neutrality Act ending the arms embargo. America could now sell arms to warring nations as long as they were paid for in cash, not through loans or gifts, and not transported by U.S. ships. To satisfy the isolationists who feared that incidents such as the *Athenia* attack would bring the United States into the war, Americans were forbidden from traveling on the ships of warring nations or to enter their ports. Not only did the lifting of the arms embargo aid the Allies, but arms production also proved to be the economic spark that lifted the U.S. economy out of the depression.

THE 1939 NEW YORK WORLD'S FAIR

There were several world's fairs held in America during the 1930s as people, despite all their problems and fears, tried to affirm their belief in the future. The fairs were also good for local economies as they created jobs and stimulated spending. The first was Chicago's World Fair of 1933–34 to celebrate that city's Century of Progress. The fair was a huge success; it drew more than 40 million spectators and made a profit on its $37 million investment. The fair was noted for its dazzling art deco architecture, which featured bold geometric designs and eye-catching colors.

The success of the Century of Progress Exposition (the other name for the Chicago World's Fair) led to fairs in Cleveland (1936), Dallas (1936), and San Francisco (1939), but the biggest of all was New York's World of Tomorrow (1939–40). The fair was built on more than 1,200 acres that had been a city dump. There were 300 buildings and 1,500 exhibitors representing 33 states and 58 countries. (Germany did not participate). More than 10,000 trees were planted as well as 1 million tulips to line its 65 miles of footpaths. The final cost was a staggering $150 million, and before it was over, 45 million people would attend.

"I made one great mistake in my life, when I signed the letter to President Roosevelt recommending that atom bombs be made."

—Scientist Albert Einstein on his part in the development of the atomic bomb

Edwin Armstrong built the first FM radio station in 1939 in New York City. His frequency modulation (FM) system produced a clearer sound than the amplitude modification (AM) system.

Visitors to the 1939 World's Fair enjoy a model of New York City. Fifty-eight nations participated in the fair, but World War II started four months after its opening. *(Library of Congress)*

The theme of the fair was the future and how technology and business would cooperate to create an efficient society in which people's lives would be much easier. One of the fair's most popular exhibits was General Motors' Futurama, which transported visitors in armchairs over a huge representation of the year 1960 in America. The exhibit included a half-million model buildings and 50,000 miniature cars, many of which moved along miniature roads. Futurama displayed an America dominated by 14-lane super highways and round cars whose speed was controlled by radio towers. However, the exhibit claimed the cars would cost only

$200. Other marvels of the future included television, robots, dishwashers, and nylon stockings.

There was also an amusement park with a 250-foot parachute jump. The most popular attraction of the entire fair, the Aquacade, involved a team of female swimmers swimming in unison to waltz music. The visual symbols of the fair were the Trylon, a 730-foot high needle-like pyramid, and the Perisphere, a 180-foot wide globe at the fair's entrance. The fair was scheduled to remain open for many years, but by the end of 1940, attendance had decreased significantly. It seemed that World War II was the only future Americans were thinking about, and the fair closed. The same site was used for the 1964–65 New York World's Fair and the symbol for that fair, the Unisphere, still stands today in Flushing Meadows Park New York.

The trylon and the perisphere were the symbols of the 1939 World's Fair as Americans tried to be hopeful about the "world of tomorrow." *(Library of Congress)*

LEISURE TIME

As unemployment remained high throughout the 1930s and unions were able to win shorter workweeks for workers, Americans' leisure time increased. Two forms of entertainment took up the vast majority of this leisure time. Millions of Americans listened to the free entertainment and news on their radios everyday, and millions went to the movies. The movies had added sound by the early 1930s, and, for just 25 cents a show, moviegoers were treated to newsreels, cartoons, serials, and two movies. By 1939, that was a deal good enough to lure an average of 100 million Americans to their neighborhood theaters every week. The decade offered

President Roosevelt moved the Thanksgiving holiday back one week in 1939. His purpose was to extend the Christmas shopping season and aid the economy.

movies in a wide variety of genres. Some films dealt with issues of the day, but most offered pure escapism, a few hours away from the problems of the real world.

Early in the decade, gangster movies were the craze. In the early gangster movies, criminals were portrayed as glamorous figures, taking advantage of a cock-eyed world and living it up. The gangsters were played by stars such as Jimmy Cagney in *Public Enemy* (1931) and Edward G. Robinson in *Little Caesar* (1930). The adulation of the movie gangster was similar to the respect such real criminals of the early 1930s as John Dillinger and Bonnie and Clyde had received. By 1934, Hollywood

Edward G. Robinson played the vicious gangster Rico in the 1930 gangster film *Little Caesar.* Robinson had a long career in Hollywood; later in his work, he usually played the good guy. *(Private Collection)*

movie producers were forced, under public pressure, to censor their films by following the Hays Code. Gangster movies continued to be popular, but the police and FBI became the good guys and the gangsters became the bad guys who had to pay for their crimes in the end.

Musicals were very popular throughout the decade, providing a large dose of escapism with their glamour and extravagance. In the first half of the decade, movie director Busby Berkeley amazed audiences with his gigantic, artistic sets and complex dance routines often involving scores of dancers. Audiences were delighted by the Berkeley top shot, in which a camera high above groups of dancers made their movements seem like a kaleidoscope of changing shapes. Berkeley movies like *42nd Street* (1933) and *Gold Diggers of 1933* (1933) mixed in a touch of realism as some songs dealt with such issues as unemployment and the struggle of the working class.

The late 1930s musical was taken over by the most famous dancing team in the history of the movies, Fred Astaire and Ginger Rogers. The couple made eight extremely successful musicals between 1934 and 1939, which were pure escapism. The movies took place in fancy nightclubs and penthouse apartments, often featuring Astaire in a tuxedo and Rogers in expensive gowns. Their flawless dancing emphasized an urban sense of elegance and sophistication, causing the viewers to lose themselves in the romance of it all.

It is not surprising that comedy movies flourished during the depression. The Marx brothers got the decade off to an uproarious start with their crazy antics. Groucho, Chico, and Harpo Marx created such chaos with their mischievous behavior, it was easy to forget that the comedies were also satires, ridiculing war in *Duck Soup* (1933), college life in *Horse Feathers* (1932) and the foolishness of the rich in *Animal Crackers* (1930).

The comedy of the Marx Brothers led directly to the uniquely 1930s screwball comedies of the second half of the decade. Screwball comedies involved ridiculous

California author John Steinbeck's *The Grapes of Wrath* was published in 1939. The book chronicles the experiences of dust bowl farmers who leave the misery of the Midwest only to find rejection and hatred in California.

Ginger Rogers and Fred Astaire were the most famous dancing team in movie history. Below they perform in *Swing Time* (1936), one of 10 films they made together. *(Private Collection)*

situations that characters struggle helplessly to control and of course make things worse along the way. What set the screwball comedy apart was the romance that was usually in the air, as a clearly ill-matched couple— often one rich and one poor—finds that love conquers

all. The best of the screwball comedies, such as *Nothing Sacred* (1937) and *Bringing Up Baby* (1938), were fast paced and showed just what the depression audience wanted to see—people having fun no matter how bad their circumstances.

Another favorite movie genre in the escapist 1930s was fantasy and horror. This genre started with the tremendous success of *Dracula* (1931), starring the eerie Bela Lugosi as the movies' most famous vampire. Many more monsters followed during the decade, including *Frankenstein* (1931) and *The Mummy* (1932) both starring Boris Karloff, and *The Invisible Man* (1933). The most popular of all the monster movies was *King Kong* (1933), although it featured a fantasy, rather than a supernatural theme. Lugosi and Karloff would

Escapism and fantasy marked many 1930s movies. In 1933, *King Kong,* the mighty ape meets his end high atop New York's Empire State Building. *(Private Collection)*

To help deal with low book sales, Pocket Books began publishing paperbacks in 1939. Americans with limited money could buy classic works of literature for as little as 25 cents each.

create many other horror roles throughout the decade, and starred together in *The Black Cat* (1935).

As great as all these films were, they were just setting the stage for 1939, when many of the greatest films Hollywood ever made were released. There was Frank Capra's *Mr. Smith Goes to Washington,* one of the best of Capra's very popular social comedies in which the idealistic common man wins over the selfish and greedy as long as the people stick together. John Wayne had his first big western hit with John Ford's *Stagecoach,* and Hollywood turned classic literature into classic film with a movie version of Emily Brontë's brooding romance *Wuthering Heights.*

Other 1939 standouts included Greta Garbo's final hit *Ninotchka; Goodbye, Mr. Chips; Beau Geste; Gunga Din; Of Mice and Men; Dark Victory;* and two of the biggest hits in the history of Hollywood *The Wizard of Oz* and *Gone With the Wind. The Wizard of Oz* was pure escapism. By 1939, American moviegoers were trying to escape both the depression and the war brewing in Europe. The musical fantasy follows the adventures of Dorothy, played by Judy Garland, and her friends the Scarecrow, the Tin Man, and the Cowardly Lion as they overcome the evil Witch of the West to help Dorothy find her way back home to Kansas. The movie has maintained its popularity with generations of children and their parents, and the song *Over the Rainbow* is a classic of American popular music.

The biggest hit of them all was *Gone With the Wind,* based on the extremely popular Margaret Mitchell 1936 best seller about the South's adversities during and after the Civil War, especially as seen through the eyes of two colorful characters, Scarlett O'Hara and Rhett Butler. The making of the film provided loads of publicity for the venture, as the producer David O. Selznick spent two years searching for the right actress to play Scarlett. He also went through two directors and several writers before the nearly four-hour production was released. Audiences loved the film, which set box-office records that stood for several decades, probably because of its theme of a defeated people rising from its darkest hour, an idea both historical and timely in 1939.

The family classic film *The Wizard of Oz* was based on an extremely popular 1900 L. Frank Baum book *The Wonderful Wizard of Oz*. *(Private Collection)*

In 1939's *Gone With the Wind,* Clark Gable and Vivien Leigh played the fiery lovers Rhett Butler and Scarlett O'Hara. *(Private Collection)*

END OF THE DECADE IN SPORTS

The depression had a serious impact on many sports during the 1930s, and game attendance dropped throughout the decade. Most sports, however, were able to maintain their popularity due to the tremendous rise of radio. By the 1930s, sports was second only to music in radio programming and provided a needed escape for a troubled nation. College football grew during the decade, adding the first four of its yearly bowl games—the Orange Bowl, Cotton Bowl, Sugar Bowl, and Sun Bowl. By the end of the decade, heavyweight champion Joe Louis was helping boxing to thrive in tough times while horse racing featured three Triple Crown winners: Gallant Fox in 1930, Omaha in 1935, and War Admiral in 1937 all won the Kentucky Derby, the Preakness Stakes, and Belmont Stakes.

The national pastime was still baseball. As the 1930s began, Babe Ruth and Lou Gehrig were the game's biggest stars, and the New York Yankees continued their domination of the sport, winning five World Series during the decade, but changes were coming. In 1935, the Cincinnati Reds installed lights at Crosley Field and played the first night game to increase attendance. It was such a success all the other Major League teams except the Chicago Cubs would install lights within the next 10 years.

The biggest change to baseball did not come until 1947, when Jackie Robinson broke the color barrier, but the seeds of integration were being planted throughout the 1930s as black players barnstormed across America showing off their skills. Legends included pitcher Satchel Paige, power hitter Josh Gibson, and speedster Cool Papa Bell. The black players held an annual all-star game at sold-out stadiums and usually beat the best white players in exhibition games held around the country. As baseball approached its 100th anniversary in 1939, it was clear that many of the black players belonged in the major leagues.

Lou Gehrig's tragic retirement on July 4, 1939, shocked the nation. Babe Ruth appeared as himself in the film version, which starred Gary Cooper as Gehrig; Gehrig himself died from amyotrophic lateral sclerosis just two years after his retirement. *(Private Collection)*

To commemorate its 100th anniversary, baseball opened its Hall of Fame in 1939 in Cooperstown, New York, the mythical birthplace of the sport. Among the first inductees were Babe Ruth, Ty Cobb, and Cy Young, but the year soon turned tragic as baseball fans learned that the game's biggest star at the time, Lou Gehrig, had to retire because of a serious illness. On July 2, before a sold-out Yankee Stadium, Gehrig gave the most famous speech in the history of sports. Despite the personal sadness of the moment, Gehrig chose instead to honor his sport and

New York Yankees rookie Joe DiMaggio racked up impressive numbers with a .323 batting average and 125 runs batted in. By 1939, he was a bright new star in Major League Baseball.

said, "Today, I consider myself the luckiest man on the face of the earth."

Gehrig died from amyotrophic lateral sclerosis, a disease that produces muscle paralysis, two years later, but as the 1930s ended, two young stars were ready to take the game into the next decade. Sluggers Joe DiMaggio of the New York Yankees and Ted Williams of the Boston Red Sox were baseball's new heroes. The torch had been passed to a new generation.

A LULL IN THE FIGHTING

After Poland's surrender in late September, Germany sat tight. German inaction led some isolationists in the United States to call the crisis the Phony War. Hitler called for a peace conference, but the Allies responded that talks could only take place after Nazi troops were removed from Poland. The Allies suspected the call for a peace conference was one of Hitler's tricks, and they were right. Hitler was actually stalling for time while he planned his invasion of France. The invasion had been scheduled for November 1939, but France had one of Europe's largest armies, and 158,000 British troops had joined them. Hitler would need the winter of 1939–40 to build up his military.

There was fighting, however, as the Soviet Union invaded Finland, a country that had been under Russian rule from 1807 to 1917. As the European war expanded in 1939, the Soviet Union wanted more protection for their important port of Leningrad near the Finland-Russia border. The Soviet Union proposed a trade of lands changing Finland's boundaries, but Finland refused. On November 30, 1939, the Soviet Union invaded Finland, an attack that included air strikes on civilians in Helsinki. British and French troops again remained in France. Roosevelt quickly denounced the invasion, and a bill was introduced in Congress to loan Finland $60 million to buy arms. By the time the bill was passed, isolationists had reduced it to $20 million for food. Without assistance, Finland could not overcome the Soviet military. Finland would be under Soviet rule by March 1940.

As 1939 was ending, Hitler was planning a spring invasion of France followed by an air invasion of England. In December, he received assurances from Major Vidkun Quisling in the Norwegian army that Quisling was planning a military coup in Norway and would help Germany occupy his Scandinavian nation. The Axis powers were meeting little resistance in their plans for world conquest. In America, President Roosevelt had finally received the authority to sell arms to the Allies, but there were few arms to sell. The depression and strong isolationism had brought arms production in America to a standstill. At the height of the depression several years before, Roosevelt had said, "This generation of Americans has a rendezvous with destiny." As a new decade dawned, it seemed to be coming true again.

On the home front, however, Americans were more concerned with everyday life than another war in Europe. As 1939 came to a close, some effects of the depression lingered on as unemployment remained over 10 percent. However, Roosevelt's New Deal had succeeded in restoring Americans' faith in their way of life and hope for the future. In a century of several activist presidents, Roosevelt was the most active. He said he wanted "to make a country in which no one is left out." This vision of America made millions of Americans feel for the first time as if they had a stake in their country.

GLOSSARY

appeasement Granting concessions to opponents to maintain peace.

appropriation Funds that have been set aside for a specific purpose.

arbitration A process for settling disputes in which two opposing sides submit their arguments to a third, objective party for a judgment.

art deco A style of decorative art known for its geometric patterns and streamlined shapes.

capitalism An economic system that calls for private ownership of the means of production, as well as the profits from production.

collective bargaining Negotiations between workers and their employers to determine issues such as wages, hours, and working conditions.

collective Ownership of an industry or a farm by the people together as a group, usually under government control.

communism A system of government in which the state controls all means of production and establishes a social order in which all goods are shared equally.

concentration camps Work prisons, especially those used by Germany's Nazi leader Adolf Hitler to persecute and eliminate Jews.

debutante A young woman making her first formal entrance into society.

dirigible An aircraft consisting of a huge bag of lighter-than-air gas, such as hydrogen or helium; a gondola, or compartment, below for carrying crew and passengers; and an engine.

embargo A suspension of trade, especially of specific goods like oil.

fascist A supporter of fascism, a system of government marked by strong control of most aspects of life by a government specifically headed by an individual, such as a dictator, which allows little personal freedom or opposition.

filibuster To delay or obstruct legislation, especially through prolonged speeches.

foreclosure The process in which a bank repossesses whatever a loan was used to buy (for example, a house, land, or a car) after repayments have not been made.

gross national product The total value of all the goods and services produced by a country during a certain amount of time.

installment buying A method of paying for a product over time; also called credit buying.

jitterbug A fast and furious dance to accompany swing music.

jukebox A large, coin-operated record player with push buttons to choose songs, usually found in restaurants and bars.

lame duck president Term that refers to a president after he loses an election but before the new president takes office.

longshoreman A worker on the docks.

margin The practice of buying stocks on credit in the stock market.

muckrakers Writers in the early 20th century who exposed social problems.

Okies Migrant farmers from the dust bowl (many from Oklahoma) who headed west after losing or abandoning their farms.

per capita Per individual.

plebiscite A vote of the entire voting population on a specific issue.

polio An infectious disease that attacks the central nervous system and produces paralysis and muscular deterioration.

profiteering Making excessive profits on goods or services that are in short supply.

Prohibition A law prohibiting the production, distribution, sale, and consumption of alcohol.

propaganda One-sided information designed to promote a cause.

recession A temporary slowdown in economic activity.

scab A worker who ignores a strike and assumes the job of a striking worker.

shantytown A section of a town or other community consisting of temporary, rundown shelters.

socialism A system of government in which production is owned and regulated by the community as a whole.

speakeasy A place where illegal alcohol was sold during Prohibition.

swing music A style of music combining elements of popular music and jazz, emphasizing a strong beat for dancing.

teamster A truck driver.

Tommy gun A Thompson submachine gun.

trickle down economics The economic theory that benefits given big business will in turn be passed down to small business and consumers.

trust A combination of businesses intended to eliminate competition.

union An alliance of workers intended to strengthen their demands for rights such as fair pay, good benefits, and safe working conditions.

FURTHER READING

BOOKS

Badger, Anthony J. *The New Deal: The Depression Years, 1933–40.* Basingstoke, England: Macmillan, 1989.

Bondi, Victor. *American Decades: 1930–1939.* Detroit, Mich.: Gale, 1995.

Brinkley, Alan. *Voices of Protest: Huey Long, Father Coughlin, and the Great Depression.* New York: Vintage, 1983.

Buhite, Russell D., and David W. Levy, eds. *FDR's Fireside Chats.* Norman: University of Oklahoma University Press, 1992.

Bullock, Alan. *Hitler and Stalin: Parallel Lives.* New York: Knopf, 1992.

Burg, David F. *The Great Depression: An Eyewitness History, Updated Edition.* New York: Facts On File, 2005.

Carroll, Peter N. *The Odyssey of the Abraham Lincoln Brigade: Americans in the Spanish Civil War.* Stanford, Calif.: Stanford University Press, 1994.

Cooney, Terry A. *Balancing Acts: American Thought and Culture in the 1930s.* New York: Twayne. 1995.

Davis, Kenneth S. *FDR: Into the Storm, 1937–1940.* New York: Random House, 1993.

———. *FDR: The New Deal Years.* New York: Random House, 1986.

Dooley, Roger. *From Scarface to Scarlett: American Film in the 1930s.* New York: Harcourt Brace, 1981.

Dudley, William, ed. *The Great Depression: Opposing Viewpoints.* San Diego, Calif.: Greenhaven, 1994.

Dulles, Foster Rhea, and Melvyn Dubofsky. *Labor in America: A History.* Arlington Heights, Ill.: Harlan Day, 1984.

Evans, Harold. *The American Century.* New York: Knopf, 1998.

Fausold, Martin L. *The Presidency of Herbert Hoover.* Lawrence: University Press of Kansas, 1985.

Feinstein, Stephen. *The 1930s: From the Great Depression to "The Wizard of Oz."* Berkeley Heights, N.J.: Enslow, 2001.

Freidel, Frank. *Franklin D. Roosevelt: A Rendezvous with Destiny.* Boston: Little, Brown, 1990.

Fremon, David K. *The Great Depression in American History.* Springfield, N.J.: Enslow. 1996.

Gallagher, Hugh Gregory. *FDR's Splendid Deception.* New York: Dodd, Mead, 1985.

Gerdes, Louise I. *The 1930s.* San Diego, Calif.: Greenhaven, 2000.

Gordon, Lois, and Alan Gordon. *American Chronicle: Year by Year Through the Twentieth Century.* New Haven, Conn.: Yale University Press, 1999.

Gregor, James N. *American Exodus: The Dust Bowl Migration and Okie Culture in California.* New York: Oxford, 1989.

Gregory, Ross. *Modern America, 1914 to 1945.* Almanacs of American Life. New York: Facts On File, 1995.

Hair, William Ivy. *The Kingfish and His Realm: The Life and Times of Huey P. Long.* Baton Rouge: Louisiana State University Press, 1991.

Hakim, Joy. *War, Peace, and All That Jazz.* New York: Oxford University Press, 1999.

Hanes, Richard C., and Sharon M. Hanes. *Historic Events for Students: The Great Depression (Vols. 1–3).* Detroit, Mich.: Gale, 2002.

Iriye, Akira. *The Origins of the Second World War in Asia and the Pacific.* New York: Longman, 1987.

Jennings, Peter, and Tod Brewster. *The Century for Young People.* New York: Doubleday, 1999.

Katz, William Loren. *The New Freedom to the New Deal: A History of Multicultural America.* Austin, Tex.: RSVP, 1993.

Kennedy, David. *Freedom from Fear: The American People in Depression and War, 1929–1945.* New York: Oxford University Press, 1999.

Kindleberger, Charles P. *The World in Depression, 1929–1939.* Berkeley: University of California Press, 1986.

Kyvig, David E. *Daily Life in the United States, 1920–1939.* Westport, Conn.: Greenwood Press, 2002.

McDonough, Frank. *Chamberlain, Appeasement, and the Road to War.* New York: Manchester University Press, 1998.

McElvaine, Robert S. *The Great Depression: America, 1929–1941.* New York: Times Books, 1995.

Miller, Nathan. *F.D.R.: An Intimate History.* New York: Doubleday, 1983.

Moser, John. *Presidents from Hoover through Truman: 1929–1953.* Westport, Conn.: Greenwood Press, 2001.

Nardo, Don. *The Great Depression.* San Diego, Calif.: Greenhaven, 1998.

Nishi, Dennis. *Life During the Great Depression,* San Diego, Calif.: Lucent, 1998.

Olson, James. *Historical Dictionary of the New Deal: From Inauguration to Preparation for War.* Westport, Conn.: Greenwood Press, 1988.

Press, Petra. *The 1930s: A Cultural History of the United States.* San Diego, Calif.: Lucent, 1999.

Rubel, David. *The United States in the 20th Century.* New York: Scholastic, 1995.

Rubinstein, W. D. *The Myth of Rescue: Why the Democracies Could Not Have Saved More Jews from the Nazis.* New York: Routledge, 1997.

Scharf, Lois, and Joan M. Jensen, *Decades of Discontent: The Women's Movement, 1920–1940.* Boston: Northeastern University Press, 1987.

Schraff, Anne E. *The Great Depression and the New Deal.* New York: Franklin Watts, 1990.

Stewart, Gail B. *The New Deal.* New York: New Discovery, 1993.

———. *Timelines: 1930s.* New York: Crestwood, 1989.

Time-Life Editors. *Hard Times: 1930–1940.* Alexandria, Va.: Time-Life, 1998.

Watkins, T. H. *The Great Depression: America in the 1930s.* Boston: Little, Brown, 1993.

Woog, Adam. *Roosevelt and the New Deal.* San Diego, Calif.: Lucent, 1998.

Wyden, Peter. *The Passionate War: A Narrative History of the Spanish Civil War, 1936–1939.* New York: Simon & Schuster, 1983.

Young, William H., and Nancy K. Young. *The 1930s: American Popular Culture through History.* Westport, Conn.: Greenwood Press, 2002.

WEBSITES

Authentic History. "1930s History and News." Available online. URL: http://www.authentichistory.com/audio/1930s/history/1930s_history_to_1937_01.html. Updated on May 3, 2005.

Digital History. "Guided Readings: 1930s." Available online. URL: http://www.digitalhistory.uh.edu/database/subtitles.cfm?titleID=69. Updated in June 2005.

Kingwood College Library. "American Cultural History, 1930–39." Available online. URL: http://kclibrary.nhmccd.edu/decade30.html. Updated in July 2001.

Virtual Library. "History, USA: 1930–1939." Available online. URL: http://vlib.iue.it/history/USA/ERAS/20TH/1930s.html. Updated on May 12, 2005.

INDEX